# Assessment in FE

## Other Titles in The Essential FE Toolkit Series

### Books for lecturers

### Books for managers

# Assessment in FE

# A Practical Guide for Lecturers

Andy Armitage and Mandy Renwick

continuum

**Continuum International Publishing Group**

| | |
|---|---|
| The Tower Building | 80 Maiden Lane, Suite 704 |
| 11 York Road | New York |
| SE1 7NX | NY 10038 |

www.continuumbooks.com

**British Library Cataloguing-in-Publication Data**
A catalogue record for this book is available from the British Library.

ISBN: 978 0 826 48738 4 (paperback/hardcover)

**Library of Congress Cataloging-in-Publication Data**
Armitage, Andy, 1950–
    Assessment in FE : a practical guide for lecturers / Andy Armitage and Mandy Renwick.
        p. cm.
    Includes bibliographical references.
    ISBN-13: 978-0-8264-8738-4 (pbk.)
    ISBN-10: 0-8264-8738-6 (pbk.)
    1. Educational tests and measurements–Great Britain. I. Renwick, Mandy. II. Title.
    LB3056.G7A76 2008
    378.1'66–dc22

                                                          2007043289

Typeset by YHT Ltd, London
Printed and bound in Great Britain by MPG Books Ltd, Cornwall

# Contents

# Series Foreword

## THE ESSENTIAL FE TOOLKIT SERIES

## Jill Jameson
## Series Editor

*In the autumn of 1974, a young woman newly arrived from Africa landed in Devon to embark on a new life in England. Having travelled halfway round the world, she still longed for sunny Zimbabwe. Not sure what career to follow, she took a part-time job teaching EFL to Finnish students. Enjoying this, she studied thereafter for a PGCE at the University of Nottingham in Ted Wragg's Education Dept. After teaching in secondary schools, she returned to university in Cambridge, and, having graduated, took a job in ILEA in 1984 in adult education. She loved it: there was something about adult education that woke her up, made her feel fully alive, newly aware of all the lifelong learning journeys being followed by so many students and staff around her. The adult community centre she worked in was a joyful place for diverse multi-ethnic communities. Everyone was cared for, including 90 year olds in wheelchairs, toddlers in the crèche, ESOL refugees, city accountants in business suits and university level graphic design students. In her eyes, the centre was an educational ideal, a remarkable place in which, gradually, everyone was helped to learn to be who they wanted to be. This was the Chequer Centre, Finsbury, EC1, the 'red house', as her daughter saw it, toddling in from the crèche. And so began the story of a long interest in further education that was to last for many years ... why, if they did such good work for so many, were FE centres so under-funded and unrecognized, so under-appreciated?*

It is with delight that, 32 years after the above story began, I write the Foreword to *The Essential FE Toolkit*, Continuum's new book series of 24 books on further education (FE) for teachers and college leaders. The idea behind the *Toolkit* is to provide a comprehensive guide to FE in a series of compact, readable books. The suite of 24 individual books are gathered together to provide the practitioner with an overall FE toolkit in specialist, fact-filled volumes designed to be easily accessible, written by experts with significant knowledge and experience in their individual fields. All of the authors have in-depth understanding of further education. But 'Why is further education important? Why does it merit a whole series to be written about it?' you may ask.

At the Association of Colleges Annual Conference in 2005, in a humorous speech to college principals, John Brennan said that, whereas in 1995 further education was a 'political backwater', by 2005 FE had become 'mainstream'. John recalled that, since 1995, there had been '36 separate government or government-sponsored reports or white papers specifically devoted to the post-16 sector'. In our recent regional research report (2006) for the Learning and Skills Development Agency, my co-author Yvonne Hillier and I noted that it was no longer 'raining policy' in FE, as we had described earlier (Hillier and Jameson 2003): there is now a torrent of new initiatives. We thought, in 2003, that an umbrella would suffice to protect you. We'd now recommend buying a boat to navigate these choppy waters, as it looks as if John Brennan's 'mainstream' FE, combined with a tidal wave of government policies will soon lead to a flood of new interest in the sector, rather than end anytime soon.

There are good reasons for all this government attention on further education. In 2004/05, student numbers in LSC council-funded further education increased to 4.2m, total college income was around £6.1 billion, and the average college had an annual turnover of £15m. Further education has rapidly increased in national significance regarding the need for ever greater achievements in UK education and skills training for millions of learners, providing qualifications and workforce training to feed a UK national economy hungrily in competition with other OECD nations. The 120 recommendations of the Foster Review (2005) therefore in the main encourage colleges to focus their work on vocational skills, social inclusion and achieving academic progress. This series is here to consider all three of these areas and more.

The series is written for teaching practitioners, leaders and managers in the 572 FE/LSC-funded institutions in the UK, including FE colleges, adult education and sixth form institutions, prison education departments, training and workforce development units, local education authorities and community agencies. The series is also written for PGCE/Cert Ed/City & Guilds Initial and continuing professional development (CPD) teacher trainees in universities in the UK, USA, Canada, Australia, New Zealand and beyond. It will also be of interest to staff in the 600 Jobcentre Plus providers in the UK and to many private training organizations. All may find this series of use and interest in learning about FE educational practice in the 24 different areas of these specialist books from experts in the field.

Our use of this somewhat fuzzy term 'practitioners' includes staff in the FE/LSC-funded sector who engage in professional practice in governance, leadership, management, teaching, training, financial and administration services, student support services, ICT and MIS technical support, librarianship, learning resources, marketing, research and development, nursery and crèche services, community and business support, transport and estates management. It is also intended to include staff in a host of other FE services including work-related training, catering, outreach and specialist health, diagnostic additional learning support, pastoral and religious support for students. Updating staff in professional practice is critically important at a time of such continuing radical policy-driven change, and we are pleased to contribute to this nationally and internationally.

We are also privileged to have an exceptional range of authors writing for the series. Many of our series authors are renowned for their work in further education, having worked in the sector for 30 years or more. Some have received OBE or CBE honours, professorships, fellowships and awards for contributions they have made to further education. All have demonstrated a commitment to FE that makes their books come alive with a kind of wise guidance for the reader. Sometimes this is tinged with world-weariness, sometimes with sympathy, humour or excitement. Sometimes the books are just plain clever or a fascinating read, to guide practitioners of the future who will read these works. Together, the books make up a considerable portfolio of assets for you to take with you through your journeys in further education. We hope the experience of reading the books will be interesting, instructive and pleasurable and that experience gained from them will last, renewed, for many seasons.

It has been wonderful to work with all of the authors and with Continuum's UK Education Publisher, Alexandra Webster, on this series. The exhilarating opportunity of developing such a comprehensive toolkit of books probably comes once in a lifetime, if at all. I am privileged to have had this rare opportunity, and I thank the publishers, authors and other contributors to the series for making these books come to life with their fantastic contributions to FE.

Dr Jill Jameson
Series Editor
March 2006

# Series introduction

What is 'assessment'? Why is it so important in the further education system? What are the most effective methods for carrying out assessments effectively with your students? Andrew Armitage and Mandy Renwick, the authors of this practical, useful guide to *Assessment in FE* explore all aspects of assessment in FE in relation to the quality of student achievement, providing a succinct, well-organized handbook that will be invaluable to all those involved in teaching and supporting student learning and achievement in post-compulsory education.

The authors discuss the selection and admission of students in the initial assessment of suitability for courses, methods of motivating students and the importance of specific, honest, positive feedback. Armitage and Renwick reinforce the need for establishing clear progression pathways for students, considering the reliability and validity of interviews as a means of assessing future potential for achievement and the use of screening, diagnostic tests and individual development plans with students. The authors help us negotiate our way around the complex assessment and qualifications frameworks in the learning and skills sector, discussing important issues relating to different examinations such as A level, the International Baccalaureate (IB), Access to HE, and vocational qualifications such as the NVQ and GNVQ.

Chapter 1 takes an overview of assessment in FE, its role, purpose and functions in the sector and the way in which measuring achievement has become more important in the selection and admission of FE students. Chapter 2 examines the content and principles involved in *what* should be assessed including frameworks for assessment and the four key concepts for assessment practice of *validity*, *reliability*, *authenticity* and *practicability*. Chapter 3 considers why and how *assessment for learning* can be used to provide learning experiences for students through the use of formative and summative feedback, based on revolutionary research by Black et al. (2003). Chapter 4 discusses *how* different techniques and methods can be used to assess students in a planned strategy for assessment, following which Chapter 5 considers *where* assessments take place, including in workplaces, simulated work environments for National Vocational Qualifications (NVQs) and in non-work curricular contexts.

Chapter 6 considers *who* carries out assessments, including tutors, assessors, workplace supervisors, learning assistants, 'unseen' examiners and students themselves in self-assessment and peer assessment. Chapter 7 discusses methods for recording and reporting achievement, providing feedback to students and filling in assignment mark sheets. Chapter 8 considers current debates about assessment in society, given the increased focus on measuring achievement, credentialism and 'the standards debate'. Chapter 9 discusses qualifications and assessment reform over the last 20 years in the context of current and future 14-19 and adult learning reforms. Following a summary of the book and a helpful overview of all chapters in Chapter 10, a thoughtful concluding section analyses key issues affecting the assessment of students in FE. These include the complexity of qualifications structures, the current confusion over progression routes for students, the debate about standards and the need for effective formative assessment methods to offer students useful learning opportunities suitable for enabling and demonstrating student achievement.

This excellent research-informed practical guide to assessment in FE will be helpful for academic, support and management staff in the learning and skills sector who need to understand the complex maze of assessment regimes and methods currently so vital to the sector. The authors, both well-known published specialists in teaching and training in post-compulsory education, have provided us with a uniquely valuable guide to assessment that powerfully and clearly outlines the key issues involved in this important area. An indispensable read.

Dr Jill Jameson
Director of Research and Enterprise
School of Education and Training
University of Greenwich

# 1: Why assess?

Most definitions of 'assessment' include the making of a decision or judgement variously about the volume, value, quality or importance of that which is being assessed. In this book, we will be concerned about the judgements of assessors with relation to the quality of student achievement in FE.

Assessment is playing an increasingly important role in the *selection and admission* of FE students. This is partly a result of colleges' realization in practice of what research has established (Martinez and Munday 1998) – that students on the wrong course are more likely to withdraw and that thorough and searching admissions procedures will have more effect on retention. The key role of formative assessment is the *giving of feedback* to students for a variety of reasons: the assessment itself can be a means of learning; students are able to monitor and improve their learning; feedback, if effectively given, can motivate students and can reinforce learning. One of the issues Curriculum 2000 and the Tomlinson proposals (DfES 2004b) attempted to address was the fragmented nature of the post-14 curriculum and the absence of clear *progression pathways* for students. The Qualification and Curriculum Authority is currently developing a Qualifications and Credit Framework and it remains to be seen whether this can help to clarify and simplify the incoherence of progression pathways. *The assessment of vocational achievement* has for the last 20 years been largely evidence-based with National Vocational Qualifications and similar awards central to measuring such achievement at five levels. In addition, a second track of more general vocational qualifications, such as GNVQ, Vocational GCSE, AVCE and, from 2005, Applied GCE AS and A, will be supplemented from 2008 onwards by 14 vocational and 3 academic diploma lines.

## Initial assessment

As a result, arguably, of funding mechanisms encouraging recruitment to particular courses and increased competition for students since incorporation, there has been pressure on colleges to recruit numbers at the expense of ensuring students are choosing courses which are appropriate to their needs and ability. In addition, widening participation and targets for expansion have led to a much broader range of students being admitted to courses so that meeting entry requirements alone is no longer a sufficient measure of whether students are suited to programmes.

The interview appears to be the key means by which student suitability is assessed. However, even though interviewers may use checklists, clear criteria and standard procedures, there are questions about the *reliability* of interviews to predict future student achievement. There are further questions about the *validity* of an interpersonal, interactive interview as a means of assessing how well a student will perform on a course demanding practical or academic skills and abilities.

---

**Task 1.1**

Find out as much as you can about the admission procedures for the courses you teach on.

- Who interviews?
- What form does the interview take – are there standard procedures?
- Is there an interview checklist or schedule?
- How far does this schedule list items covered/information given/received, and how far does it require an evaluative judgement on the part of the interviewer?
- Is there hidden assessment – do interviewers draw conclusions from the way the application form is completed for example?

---

**Task 1.2**

Find out what you can from your students about their views on the admissions experience they had.

- What element of assessment do they think there was?
- Did it, in their view, effectively measure their suitability for the course they are now taking?

Many colleges are now routinely testing applicants. Although such testing may be to supplement admissions interviews above, they are increasingly being used for screening and diagnostic purposes. Screening is backward – looking at attempts to gauge a student's achievement and level of ability. Diagnostic assessment is forward – looking at its role in determining a learner's potential and the likely learning needs which will have to be addressed. Such diagnostic assessment may also have a guidance purpose, may be part of an induction process and be linked to the drawing up of an individual development plan. A guide to initial assessment (DfEE 2001) suggests learner information to be considered during initial assessment might be as follows:

- *career preferences* and aspirations;
- *qualifications and achievements* which can give an indication of the students' strengths and weaknesses but particularly with regard to the level of qualification which may be suitable for them;
- *ability and potential* which may not be indicated in the actual qualifications they hold;
- *prior learning and experience* which students may have had through achievement of units/modules rather than whole qualifications or vocational skills and knowledge already acquired in the workplace;
- *basic and key skills* levels, particularly in Communications, Application of Number, ICT;
- *learning difficulties*, which may include specific learning difficulties not previously recognized;
- *information* about interests and hobbies may be useful for vocational guidance purposes or in devising personalized learning which engages the student;
- *learning styles* inventories and questionnaires are increasingly being used to identify individual styles (www.support4learning.org.uk is a website giving comprehensive information on learning styles, while Coffield et al.

(2004) provide a critical appraisal of key measures of learning styles);

- information about a student's *job role*, where relevant, will be central in determining how far college and workplace will offer the opportunities for the learning and practice of occupational skills and abilities;
- skills such as self-confidence, reliability, problem solving, indicate a student's overall *personal effectiveness*;
- there may be aspects of a student's *personal circumstances* such as medical conditions or child-care responsibilities which need to be taken into consideration for learning opportunities to be maximized.

---

**Task 1.3**
Consider how far the initial assessment of your students gained information relating to the aspects above.

---

## Motivating and providing feedback to learners on progress

Providing effective feedback to students that is supportive of their learning and development is a key purpose of formative assessment. The work of Paul Black and colleagues with a group of teachers (Black et al. 2003) used Ruth Butler's findings in developing innovative strategies for giving feedback by marking (Butler 1988). Butler had found that comment-only feedback had a more positive effect on student learning than marks-only feedback or a combination of marks and comments. Using marks-only feedback in a variety of different ways, Black's teachers found that 'Comments should identify what has been done well and what still needs improvement and give guidance on how to make improvements' and that 'Opportunities for students to follow up comments should be planned as a part of the overall learning process'.

Feedback, then, should be specific, identifying what has been done well by the individual student and what needs improving. It should also be timely, given as soon as is practicable after the task to be assessed in order to be most effective. It should be realistic – setting developmental targets that students can achieve. And it should be honest about what has been achieved so far and what needs to be achieved. Feedback should be positive and supportive: too often we focus, as assessors, on the shortcomings of a piece of work, underestimating the potency of such feedback in affecting students' self-esteem (Gipps 1994, pp. 129–36). Students who were part of Black's study were concerned that their teachers wrote legibly so that comments could be read and that the teachers provided comments that they could understand.

---

**Task 1.4**

Select a piece of work you have recently marked. Evaluate your assessment as to how far it was:

- Specific
- Timely
- Realistic
- Honest
- Legible
- Comprehensible, clear and unambiguous.

---

Assessment for learning will be revisited in Chapter 3.


## Assessment for progression

Assessing achievement at a series of levels only goes part of the way to facilitating student progression. Although students graduating to AS and A2 from GCSE appear to be following a clear academic route from Levels 2 to 3, they may find the transition uneven and lacking in progression in terms of content, breadth and the nature of the courses themselves. More uneven still can be the transition from or to academic and vocational courses and it was for this reason that the mixed package of an academic/vocational programme envisaged as part of Curriculum 2000 did not materialize for most, with students still following by and large an academic or vocational route.

The revision of the National Qualification Framework in 2004 with qualifications recognized at one of eight levels, provides some indication of the skills, attributes, processes and accountability required at each level. The Qualifications and Curriculum Authority is currently developing a Qualification and Credit Framework. The difference from the current framework (NQF) will be that it will be a unit-based credit system. This will allow students to build up towards and transfer credits to a qualification. The Framework will recognize the volume or quantity of achievement as well as the level. Together with a range of rules of combination this should enable progression from one qualification to another to be clearer and more flexible.

The A level has for many years acted as the principal means of selection for higher education. However, many universities are now doubting the A level's usefulness as a selection tool amid claims of grade inflation.

'A crisis of confidence in the A-level is fuelling a three-fold increase in the number of schools offering the International Baccalaureate (IB).

The International Baccalaureate Organization says that the number of schools offering the IB has increased from 34 in 2000 to 85, and is expected to exceed 100 next year. State schools have now overtaken private schools, with 51 offering the diploma.

As a steady stream of well-respected schools embrace the alternative to A-levels, fears have been heightened that the "gold standard" A-level is in terminal decline.

A further blow was dealt to the beleaguered qualification last week when research by Durham University appeared to provide compelling evidence that A-levels are getting easier. The data, compiled by Robert Coe, of the university's Curriculum, Evaluation and Management Centre, shows that students are now achieving up to three grades higher at A-level than those of similar ability in the 1980s.

The research, which gives 200,000 sixth formers an ability test every year, shows that average candidates who got an F in A-level mathematics in 1988 would have got a C last year.

Average students in biology and geography, who in 1988 would have got an E, would have got a C in 2005.

Anthony Seldon, the master of Wellington, told the *Sunday Telegraph*: "There is a crisis of confidence in the current exam system. A-levels have some good features but they do not sufficiently stretch some young people. Universities are voting with their feet and introducing their own admission exams and this is sending out the message to schools that A-levels are not good enough."

Mr Seldon, who will host a conference this week on alternatives to A-level, is calling for a Royal Commission into England's "failing" exam system. "You need an exam that encourages good teaching and learning, independent thinking and distinguishes the intellectually able from the merely well drilled," he said. "A-level is not doing any of that. The Government have known this for a long time and we have waited and waited for something to be done."

The IB has been offered in the United Kingdom since the 1970s but has proved increasingly popular with schools and universities since 2000, when the Government changed the A-level into a two-part qualification with unlimited resits.'

(Henry 2006)

The International Baccalaureate (from 2008) is only one of 18 qualifications or groups of qualifications recognized by the UCAS tariff for entry to higher education, which range from British Horse Society Stage 3 Horse Knowledge & Care, Stage 3 Riding and Preliminary Teacher's Certificate (from 2008 entry onwards) to CACHE Diploma In Child Care and Education, to Music Examinations at grades 6, 7 and 8, as well as GCE AS/A level. There is no firm evidence that any particular route is likely to be a better preparation for university study than others but there is some suggestion that Access and GNVQ courses require students to be more self-directed and less teacher dependent and therefore better equipped to deal with university study.

> **Task 1.5**
> In groups, share your knowledge of Level 3 programmes. Consider how these are assessed and the extent to which that assessment might inform you and those in HE about students' ability to study at HE level.

The role of qualifications in selection for higher education and employment will be discussed extensively in Chapter 8.

## Assessing professional/vocational skills and achievement

National Vocational Qualifications (NVQ) and similar awards measure achievement in the following vocational areas:

- Tending animals, plants and land
- Extracting and providing natural resources
- Construction
- Engineering
- Manufacturing
- Transportation
- Providing goods and services
- Providing business services
- Communicating
- Developing and extending knowledge and skills.

NVQs comprise series of units, each containing elements with associated assessment criteria, developed in relation to national occupational standards. Each of these specifies skills or competencies framed in 'can do' statements. Candidates are required to produce a range of evidence indicating that they can demonstrate such competencies. This demonstration should be completed ideally in a workplace context. Assessment should take place when the candidate is ready to be assessed and they are able to complete tasks more than once to do this. Indeed, with some forms of evidence, such as direct observation, they may be required to demonstrate the competence on more than one occasion to satisfy the assessor that they are competent.

Armitage et al. (2007) suggest that the debate about evidence-based assessment revolves around several issues: first, that it is unable to distinguish between levels of performance – a competence is a competence; second, that the assessment of competencies emphasizes the assessment of public performance rather than cognitive achievement; third, that evidence-based approaches make learning assessment led with a narrow focus on competencies, the gathering of evidence and its assembly in portfolios rather than its quality. Finally, there are some concerns about evidence-based assessment regarding both its validity and reliability. The validity of assessment relates to how effectively and appropriately it measures what it claims to; for example, some argue the driving tests (both theory and practice) are only valid tests of the ability to pass the tests, not of the ability to drive. Reliability concerns the capacity of assessment to measure achievement consistently, in different conditions, at different times, with varying groups of students and assessors. The concepts of 'validity' and 'reliability' are considered in detail in Chapter 2.

---

**Task 1.6**

Below are listed some of the key NVQ assessment methods. Discuss the potential strengths and weaknesses with regard to validity and reliability of each in relation to assessing one demonstration of vocational skill described below:

a) Provide manicure treatment
b) Develop and maintain a healthy, safe and secure environment for patients
c) Produce effective working drawings for a book jacket design
d) Keep stock at required levels
e) Work effectively with colleagues in a retail environment.

NVQ assessment methods:

- Direct observation of practice by an assessor or supervisor
- Candidate's reflection
- Work products
- Expert witness testimony

- Case study
- Oral questioning
- Professional discussion
- Service user testimony
- Written assignment
- Simulation/role play.

The NVQ was always intended as an award not as a course, but in spite of this NVQs are run in a variety of settings including FE colleges, raising issues of reliability. As Torrance et al. found:

'What one might call "opportunities to verify" vary greatly across work-based and college-based settings. For example, small garages may not provide NVQ 3 opportunities to conduct diagnostic work with the latest computer technology. Equally, however, and, somewhat ironically, well-resourced main dealers for leading car makers do not always provide NVQ Level 2 opportunities for basic repair.'

(Torrance 2005)

Some have queried the mantra that workplace-based assessment is the most appropriate context for the measurement of vocational skills. An in-service student on a teacher training programme who managed the training in a string of hair salons investigated why student achievement on their salon-based NVQ was not what she expected it to be. She found that the stylists, who were supervising the trainees, were often not the most effective at doing so: excellent stylists do not necessarily have the communication and observation skills to fulfil the supervisory role.

One of the reasons for the introduction of competence-based assessment of vocational learning and achievement was to remove the theory/practice dualism of previous vocational programmes, in which the theory was completed at college on day release and the practical skills developed in the workplace. There is some doubt about whether the theory/practice division has been consigned to history. The authors recently observed a session in a motor vehicle workshop: after an hour working on engines in the workshop, the students washed thoroughly, took off their overalls and climbed the stairs to the classroom for an hour of theory!

# 2: What to assess – content and principles

The many reasons why we assess student learning have been identified. In this chapter we look at *what* to assess. This involves a consideration of what can be called a *framework* for assessment and how assessment relates to the aims and objectives established for a particular learning experience, either through lesson plans, schemes of work, syllabuses or award body specifications. It is essential to have a referencing system for any assessment exercise and thus decisions have to be made about the appropriateness of *comparisons* and whether they are to be made with the performance of other students (norm-referencing), against set criteria (criterion-referenced) or self-referencing (ipsative assessment).

One of the most important principles in assessment practice is that of *validity*. An exploration of this principle focuses on how validity in assessment processes is ensured, that is, how the methods used to assess learning really do measure whatever they are supposed to measure and no more or no less! Once again this can be related back to the objectives or learning outcomes, where content, process and product – often a blend of all three – are being assessed.

Another important principle in framing the organization of an assessment strategy is that of *practicability* – the capacity to carry out the most suitable form of assessment in the circumstances which are provided, since inability to do this can jeopardize a well-designed assessment framework. Linked to this is *authenticity* – the issue of whether a sufficiently real context for assessing performance can be achieved through the tasks chosen for assessment purposes.

How can fairness in assessment be assured? *Equality* in assessment is an ever-increasingly important issue. The growth in individualized learning presents a challenge of differentiated assessment, combined with a need to guarantee that assessors are not influenced by class, gender or cultural factors in their roles. *Reliability* in the assessment process increases the potential for all students to benefit from a framework which is maximized in terms of its reliability through specific performance criteria, rigorous marking schemes and sound modification and verification processes.

## A framework for assessment

Creating a framework for assessment is about establishing a referencing system, which, in its broadest scope, allows an effective, fair and transparent assessment of what a student has learned. Clearly, a starting point for such decisions is the interrelationship between what has been learned (or assumed to have been learned) and what will be assessed. While this may seem obvious as a concept to teachers, it is not always apparent to their students and sometimes with good reason! For the experience or impression of having been 'tested' unfairly in some manner while at school or college on an aspect of learning is familiar to many. This might have come about as a result of ignorance about good assessment practice; occasionally, through carelessness. It ranges from very serious and publicly reported cases, such as students being examined in subjects not covered in the syllabus they have been taught as a result of tutors having misread that syllabus, to poorly constructed assessment questions and cases where the ambiguity of language used to articulate the questions confuses the respondent. Put simply, assessment should enable the measurement of achievement in learning against criteria. If there are no criteria, then there are no terms of reference with which to make assessment as a process meaningful. If the criteria are expressed in a jargon which is so inaccessible for students, as has sometimes been the case with NVQ programmes, then this can disadvantage students hugely. Assessment criteria enable judgements and comparisons to be made about the quality of a student's learning. According to Rowntree, there are three questions that need to be asked in relation to criteria. They are:

1   How well has the student done by comparison with (predetermined) criteria?
2   How well have they done by comparison with peers?
3   How well have they done compared with their own past performance?

(Adapted from Rowntree 1987, pp. 178–9)

---

**Task 2.1**

Think about the ways in which you have been assessing a group of students. Comment on the way in which the judgements you have made enabled you to:

1   consider students' performance against set criteria
2   compare individual performance among the group
3   compare individual students' recent performance with their past endeavours.

---

The first of these questions concerns criterion-referenced assessment and is a commonly recognized frame of reference in FE colleges today, for it is the type of assessment largely underpinning vocational qualifications. Appropriate criteria are established by awarding and professional bodies for assessment purposes and successful achievement is dependent upon meeting those criteria. Criterion-referenced assessment is popular for a number of reasons:

- in theory it is objective, although this depends on the specificity and clarity of the criteria
- students are not competing against each other to achieve – discrimination is likely therefore to be minimal.

Criterion-referenced assessment, however, is not without its problems or critics. Being specific and unambiguous in the expression of criteria is not always easy, as what is clear to one person is less so to another. An awarding body may set the criteria, which then have to be explained and interpreted by a teacher for a student. If criteria are in any way open to interpretation or are vague, then the achievement of performance is unreliable.

Norm-referenced criteria, which relate to question 2, are

useful when one of the chief purposes of assessment is selection, that is, determining individual performance of students in comparison with each other. The most notable example of this in the FE sector is public examinations, where results are used to decide suitability for university entrance. The emphasis has shifted away from the achievement of a threshold level or standard in criterion-referenced assessment to an interest in grades – in other words to the level at which a student has performed within a range of qualitative scores. To some degree, the questionability of norm-based criteria lies at the core of the current debate about university entrance, for one argument is about whether students from certain socio-economic back-grounds are disadvantaged under such an assessment regime through a combination of poorer schooling and/or low self-expectations. This issue will be examined in greater depth in Chapter 8. As Rowntree points out (1987, p. 185), norm- and criterion-referenced assessment are to some degree more similar than they first appear to be. For in order to establish assessment criteria there is a tendency to look at the achievements of past groups of students. If these achievements are not taken into account, then criteria may be set at too high or too low a level. The result of this tendency, however, is that what appears to be criterion-referenced is often actually norm-referenced – a process recognizable on an annual basis in the suspected adjustment of A level grades.

Ipsative, or self-referenced assessment, is the form of assessment over which a student has complete control and, arguably, is one in which they have more interest. It is normally referred to as self-assessment. Self-assessment is gaining in importance, since it is linked to the concept of assessment for learning, which will be explained in depth in the following chapter.

All too often the practice of assessment is an area of mystery to students, because it has not been explained to them. They have been told what to do to *complete* an assessment, but this is not the same as understanding *why* they are doing it. Assumptions that criteria, syllabuses and specifications are readily comprehensible can lead to major problems if the students do not know what they are working towards. And if they do not know this, then they are likely to achieve only on a 'hit and miss' basis!

## Assessment principles

There are four key principles which every teacher needs to know about assessment practice. These are validity, reliability, authenticity and practicability. A starting principle for setting criteria is that of validity. The meaning of validity in assessment practice is not obvious. Synonyms for *valid* in everyday speech are 'alright' or 'OK'. One student in a PGCE PCET group said recently that her assessment practice was valid because it was genuine and acceptable. But what did she mean by this? To say that our assessment practice is 'alright' or 'acceptable' carries no meaning at all. This is, after all, a subjective judgement! So, the precise meaning of the word in educational assessment terms has to be learned. If an assessment process is valid, this means that it measures what it is supposed to measure. Validity is about making sure that the student has learned what they are supposed to have learned and so assessment can be said to be valid only if it is set alongside learning outcomes. This, however, is a very simple definition of validity.

For there are different types of validity, and Tummons (2005, pp. 46–7) offers a clear definition of the five types: face validity, content validity, construct validity, predictive validity and validity through authenticity. In this chapter the focus will be on face, construct and content validity,

How, then, can we be sure that assessment techniques measure what they are supposed to measure effectively? As already stated, valid assessment processes are those which measure how well students have met the objectives set for a programme of learning. These objectives are also known as 'learning outcomes' – a phrase which makes the link between learning and assessment clearer. To set valid assessment tasks therefore requires a careful consideration of each learning outcome and how it might be measured. And this demonstrates in fact the importance of having SMART objectives, that is, those that are specific, measurable, appropriate, relevant and timely, as these will be more easily translatable into specific assessment tasks. Learning outcomes specify the knowledge, skills and understanding expected of a student as a result of an individual lesson or a programme of studies. Sometimes these are expressed as competencies, where a level or standard of performance is expected, as in vocational training. Assessment tasks should enable a student to demonstrate that the knowledge, skills and understanding, or a blend of two or three of these as expressed in the learning outcomes or objectives, have been learned. This might involve showing that a product has arisen as a result of the learning experience or that process learning has taken place.

---

**Task 2.2**

Take a set of learning outcomes from a course you teach. Take each outcome and analyse it in terms of what the student is expected to have achieved from the learning. Then, from the outcomes, devise formative assessment tasks to measure the knowledge, skills and understanding emerging from the outcomes.

Take, for example, an outcome from a Level 2 NVQ module in support services in health care, that: 'by the end of the course students will be able to give clients appropriate food and drink'.

Formative assessment tasks to measure achievement of this competence might include: monitoring how students collect information from their clients and their carers, encouraging them to keep notes about how clients react to different foods and drinks, question and answer, and quizzes.

---

Often the performance indicators that yield useful indications of what has been learned will be very specific. This can be important in learning with a product-oriented outcome. On some of the popular cookery programmes on television, for example, trainee chefs or celebrities will watch a demonstration of a dish being made and then be assessed on their observational learning, and ability to apply that learning, through having to produce the same dish themselves. Sometimes a time limit is imposed on the activity, requiring the novice to work under the same conditions and pressure that they would encounter if they were in a real-life restaurant situation. So the contestants are working to produce a dish to a certain standard (i.e. that set by the chef during the demonstration phase) within a set time limit (i.e. one which matches the speed at which a chef might have to work in a restaurant). These are very specific and readily measurable criteria.

In other types of learning, however, process might be an important factor in determining progress. This is often in learning situations where learning is not easily measured within a very specific timeframe and is perhaps more complex, unlike the media example. Learning to drive a car is an example. If learning to drive was simply about acquiring a set of ma-noeuvres, then most people would learn very quickly. It is, however, a much more complex learning process involving combining the acquisition of practical skills with road aware-ness, confidence and a knowledge of the Highway Code, which is tested separately. The summative practical test is cri-terion-referenced and examiners are testing a range of skills and attitudes during the test itself, but frequently drivers are heard to say that they only really learned to drive *after* passing their test. In other words, a real assessment of their driving, in their view, is not what happens within the specific timeframe of the test itself, but in the years to follow. This is recognition of the importance of process in the learning experience and many people's evaluation of their driving would be that a more genuine assessment of their skills might extend beyond the one hour test on the road.

A very different example of assessing process is in the development of study skills among FE students. Often this is assessed through tasks specific to an area of study. Take time management, for example. This cannot be measured as easily through using SMART targets and as a skill it is measured over quite a long period of time. It is important for all students as a prerequisite for successful study and is most effectively meas-ured through self-assessment. The study skills that enable achievement of assessment tasks include: presentational and written communication skills; strategies for effective reading and note-taking; time management; and revision techniques. Tutors will add to this list according to the level and type of students they have. Acquisition of these skills is built over the period of a programme and beyond, often with the support of a tutor, online tutorials and through feedback. Many programmes assess these skills in their own right.

Validity is a hallmark of a sound assessment strategy in a competence-based learning system, since assessment is supposed to be rooted in authentic workplace tasks and therefore reflect the reality and demands of a particular profession. Evidence suggests, however, that some learning contexts fall short of the ideal in that, for a range of reasons, mainly concerning a lack of resources and a shortage of workplace settings, students on NVQ programmes are not always offered entirely valid assessment experiences (Torrance 2005, pp. 58–9). This in turn means that some of the assessment scenarios have to be simulated within a college environment; the institution may also have a problem replicating valid assessment processes for resource reasons. This then substantially undermines the ethos of competence-based assessment, giving rise to employer criticism that students are not well prepared for the world of work. Funding realities mean that this is a difficult issue for colleges, since money for adequate resources is often in short supply.

Valid assessment tasks should be aspirational, for assessment practice is about finding an ideal framework for seeing what learning has taken place and making it authentic.

What is meant by authenticity? It has two meanings in assessment language. One is the issue of whether the task can be carried out in the circumstances under which it would be carried out in everyday life. The first aspect of authenticity then relates to the context in which the assessment takes place and the degree to which the assessment exercise simulates what would be required of a candidate in a real life situation. Taking the example of a practical skill being assessed, does the task require that the student complete the skill not just within a realistic context but also within a given timeframe? If, for example, a student were allowed 15 minutes to successfully remove the cork from a bottle of wine, this would not accurately reflect the pressure she might be under to perform that task in a busy restaurant on a Saturday night! Here the link between authenticity and validity can be seen.

## Authenticity and practicability

For assessment to be effective it must be authentic, especially within a vocational context. The simulation of an actual working context can be difficult within a college environment for a number of reasons. First, there may not be the capacity in terms of space to reproduce an authentic working environment. This will affect teaching, learning and assessment. It may be, for example, that lack of space minimizes the hazards that the normal working environment would pose, so that during an assessment it is difficult to measure how well a candidate might cope were the environment to match a real working environment more closely. This can make formative assessment exercises carried out in the college problematic. Another reason may be issues concerning availability of materials and equipment that are up to date and in sufficiently abundant quantities to allow for assessment of all students – this is frequently a problem in FE colleges, where funding is limited. This may then limit the practicability of assessment arrangements, making them burdensome for tutors who are trying to juggle validity and authenticity with practical issues such as lack of time, equipment and a limited team of tutors to carry out a sometimes large number of assessments. If due attention is not given to the importance of practicability, the assessment regime may be compromised.

## Reliability and equality in assessment

Like the term 'validity', reliability has a very specific definition in assessment language. It is a twinned principle with validity in the sense that the absence of either reliability or validity weakens the effectiveness of the assessment process considerably. Essentially, reliability is to do with fairness and ensuring that assessment processes offer maximum fairness for all who are being assessed. Where validity is concerned with measuring what it is supposed to measure, reliability is about the consistency of that measurement (Petty 2004, p. 322), and there are several factors which contribute to guaranteeing that consistency. These are:

- a specific and unambiguous articulation of performance criteria and descriptors
- carefully thought through marking schemes
- rigorous, frequent and transparent moderation and verification practices
- staff training to ensure that all of the above are carried out.

The first of these is related to planning, which should take place well in advance of an actual assessment event. If the performance indicators of a competence-based programme are expressed in readily understandable terms, then there is an increased possibility that they are not open to interpretation. It is for this reason that course planning should always be a shared process, so that ideally all those who will eventually teach on a programme have commonality of understanding in relation to descriptors and indicators and that these are discussed thoroughly and agreed upon before publication. Once agreed, these must be adhered to rigidly and applied objectively. The idea of 'easy' and' hard' markers, which is familiar to us all, should never arise! Of course, it is not always possible to be part of the team that developed a course, and this is where the introduction to performance descriptors must be explained carefully to new members of staff during induction. Specificity in the marking criteria should ease the award of appropriate grades. This should mean that if several markers are all looking at one candidate's performance they will award the same grade. If the award band is narrow, such as PASS or FAIL, this can be straightforward, except in cases where some markers are hovering over a 'borderline' case. Of course it is only in such situations that the decisions to pass or fail a candidate are ever discussed! Paradoxically, the more complex the marking scheme, the greater variety there is likely to be for the markers in awarding the same grade, despite apparently clear criteria and narrow marking bands. And sometimes it is when disagreements arise during moderation exercises about awarding a grade that the in-depth discussions about those descriptors and grades which should have preceded the marking process really begin to take place! Almost inevitably, it is during summative and not formative assessment processes that attention is paid to reliability. This, however, is a normal part of the cycle of curriculum development and is part of the process of refining the assessment elements of programmes. Tummons also points out that just because two markers agree a common grade, this is not necessarily the result of their having both followed the same assessment criteria. Arriving at the same conclusion could simply be 'a reflection of the fact that those two examiners both have similar standards in relation to the assessment' (Tummons 2005, p. 52).

Ensuring fairness to students in the assessment process also includes practical considerations about consistent practices among staff in relation to individual students. Differentiated assessment practice may be a laudable phenomenon, but it can lead to some tricky situations, where particular students may be seen to be being treated favourably over others on account of special circumstances. Two examples of how reliability may be reduced are in extra assistance and deadlines. The first is about an issue of the dividing line between what work has been produced by the student him- or herself and the help they may have received from a tutor or even another adult in producing that work. Weak students may require extra assistance to help them pass a certain assessment. If they do not receive such help, then there may be accusations of lack of support. At the same time, support to students should be concrete and *enabling*, and this can often spill over into a prescriptive type of assistance, in which the hand of the tutor is apparent. Extensions of deadlines is an ever-complex issue, proven by the fact that in the last few years there has been an increase in the demand for *evidence* to support requests for extension deadlines. The issue of extensions, however, raises questions about flexibility within a learning process to allow students to achieve 'in their own time'. But at what point is it fair to allow one student extra time to complete a piece of work and perhaps earn a better grade than another student who has respected the deadline, but who would also have performed better with a greater time allowance? Deliberating on these questions of fairness can be very time-consuming. It is a good idea therefore to have established parameters, in print, and to ask students to 'sign up' to agreeing to fair principles for all. Consistency is also about all staff following the same ground rules and not disapplying them through a whim or personal motive.

---

**Task 2.3**

Look back now at the assessment tasks you devised for Task 2.2 and examine them in terms of validity and reliability. How could you improve the tasks in these terms?

---

When considering the notion of equality in assessment practice, several factors must be examined. The notion itself extends into different realms, usually those to do with access and inclusion, but an overriding principle governing equality in assessment in whatever circumstances is fairness to all. Translating access and inclusion into assessment practice involves a clear understanding of the elements of the existing practice which can be maintained and those which cannot.

Furthermore, making amendments to existing practice means that the principles of validity and reliability which have already been examined will need to be at the forefront of such considerations and that alternative assessment strategies are 'genuine' (Robson 2005, p. 84). Robson claims that there is considerable evidence of poorly formed alternative assessment strategies, where a measured approach is called for (2005, p. 87). This involves trialling different forms of alternative assessments to evaluate their effectiveness. The goal is to move away from 'compliance' with the legal requirement, under the Disability Discrimination Act (DDA), towards 'change embraced for the value perceived' (Follet 2003, cited in Robson 2005).

Special Educational Needs and Disability Act (SENDA) guidelines on fair assessment practice focus on making changes to keep it within the law, but also in an 'anticipatory manner' – a proactive, rather than reactive, policy. As Race points out, this is challenging:

'This is a tricky situation, as in one sense the purpose of assessment is to *discriminate* between learners, and to find which learners have mastered the syllabus the best, the least, and so on. If we're honestly discriminating in terms of ability, that might be lawful. But if we're discriminating in terms of disability, it won't be lawful. But aren't they the same thing? Where does ability stop and disability begin?'

(Race 2005, p. 75)

The theme of *fairness to all* is also applicable to another aspect of assessment practice: plagiarism and collusion. These considerations form what might be termed the 'negative' aspects of practice. They are about eradicating forms of unfair advantage which students buy into in order to falsely claim success and certification. Nothing threatens to undermine assessment as a learning tool as much as this form of cheating. Unfortunately, it is becoming a very popular means of getting good marks and grades, and is fuelled by a booming net business. The teacher's role in plagiarism and collusion is one of quick action, objectivity and neutrality, as it is the under-detection of these two which is a threat to fairness. To some degree it is true to say that it is academic more than vocational programmes in FE which are the more adversely affected, since the assessment of some aspects of competence for the latter is often via observational tasks. Examples of plagiarism are varied, but the most common forms are:

- copying verbatim from a published source without attribution
- copying and or adapting part of another student's work without permission
- asking another person to complete the assessment task, sometimes paying for such a service
- falsely claiming extra time under 'mitigating circumstances' for completion of a task.

Tutors may, wittingly or otherwise, collude in such practice through:

- demonstrating inconsistency in dealing with cases of plagiarism
- giving some students the 'benefit of the doubt' if pressures of time mean that thorough checking is difficult
- being tougher on brighter students

- failing to ensure that students are clear on what constitutes plagiarism.

There are serious forms of cheating which menace the 'fairness for all' principle. QCA reported a figure of 16 per cent of pupils found guilty of a form of cheating in the 2006 GCSE and A level examinations. Apart from plagiarism and collusion this included pupils who had used mobile telephones to assist them to cheat and used unauthorized material in the examination room (Andalo 2007).

A review will also need to be made of how adjustments to established practice affect both formative and summative assessment. In the case of the latter it is often necessary to contact the awarding body to seek approval for planned modifications (Tummons 2005, p. 122). Tummons has produced an invaluable checklist for FE practitioners to assist in evaluating the planning of both formative and summative processes (2005 pp. 124–8). These lists are relevant to the formulation of an assessment framework for students with a wide range of learning difficulties. In general, the adaptations to existing formative assessment practice are those which would already have been made within the classroom; it is those made to summative processes which require more careful planning to include adequate time in advance of the formal assessment event to communicate with the external awarding bodies.

In establishing a framework for assessment, the process of formulating appropriate tasks is seemingly straightforward, involving the use of objectives and learning outcomes. There are, however, important principles of assessment practice which must be taken into consideration, as well as individual differences that require a differentiated approach. Only if these principles are adhered to will valid and reliable measurements of progress and achievement be achieved.

# 3: Assessment for learning

The central concerns of this chapter are the purposes and uses of assessment as a learning experience for students. This is known as 'assessment for learning'. Chapter 1 established the importance of the process of assessment in motivational terms and underlined the function of assessment as a guide for progression. Chapter 3 will focus more specifically on the way in which assessment should be harnessed to motivation through providing feedback on student work that allows that learner to make progress. The phrase 'for learning' may seem obvious. Until recent years, however, there has been an emphasis on the assessment 'of' learning, that is, on summative achievement, which has often been at the expense of the formative assessment process that helps the learner to progress towards these summative goals. The ground-breaking work of Black et al. (2003), referred to in Chapter 1, largely responsible for focusing greater attention on assessment for learning throughout UK education, will be looked at in the section 'Assessment for learning'. 'Planning a formative strategy' will concentrate on the differences between *formative* and *summative* assessment and consider the need to *plan* a formative assessment strategy. The communication of clear assessment criteria to students is explored in 'Explaining assessment criteria' and in 'Linking formative assessment to personal development planning' the role of assessment feedback in personal development planning is analysed for its contribution to student learning.

The concept of assessment for learning has been promoted vigorously by major educational groups in the last few years and in 2002 the *Assessment Reform Group* established ten principles to underpin classroom practice They are as follows:

1 Assessment for learning should be part of effective planning of teaching and learning.
2 It should focus on how students learn.
3 It should be recognized as central to classroom practice.
4 Assessment for learning should be regarded as a key professional skill for teachers.
5 This process should be sensitive and constructive on account of its emotional impact.
6 Assessment should take account of the importance of learner motivation.
7 It should promote commitment to learning goals and create a shared understanding of the criteria by which they are assessed.
8 Learners should receive constructive feedback about how to improve.
9 Assessment for learning develops learners' capacity for self-assessment so that they can become reflective and self-managing.
10 Assessment for learning should recognize the full range of achievements of all learners.

Many of these principles are implicit in the practice promoted throughout this book, but we will look specifically at them in greater detail in this chapter.

## Assessment for learning

The research carried out by Black and Wiliam (1998) created a revolution in the manner in which assessment is viewed today. Rowntree (1987) had already paved the way for such research with his observations on the key distinctions between formative and summative processes. These observations were radical in the sense that they shifted the focus from 'form' in assessment theory onto one of 'intention'. By formalizing these distinctions Rowntree introduced the notion of formative assessment as a practice to support and enhance student achievement. In short, he refocused the purpose of assessment onto the principle of assessment *for* learning, as opposed to one of simply a meas-urement *of* learning. Black and Wiliam's work has concentrated on the student's understanding of the formative assessment strategy and the teacher's responsibility and role in formulating this understanding. The focus is also on an appreciation of the rewards which result from this strategy for both teacher and student. Teachers have a greater awareness of how effective their strategies are and can therefore support students better, while the students themselves have a greater capacity in theory for self-development.

Black et al.'s research led them to determine four types of action that can make for a worthwhile formative assessment strategy. These are outlined fully in Chapter 4 of their book *Assessment for Learning* (Black et al. 2003). The four types are:

- questioning
- feedback through marking
- peer and self-assessment
- the formative use of summative tests.

The subject of feedback through marking is discussed in detail in Chapter 7, and Chapter 6 contains information on peer and self-assessment. Investigating the method of questioning involved a significant emphasis on 'wait time' as a technique – the idea that by increasing the amount of time between posing a question and often intervening to answer our own questions (!) could benefit students by allowing them time to think about an answer. Teachers who were part of Black et al.'s research discovered that changing their technique to allow more time for answers, allowing students to comment on their peers' responses before moving to fresh questions, and using carefully formulated questions, rather than those created on an ad-hoc basis, led to a better level of enquiry and discussion within the classroom (2003, pp. 33–6).

Research looking at the formative use of summative tests revealed the benefits of students setting their own questions and marking others' answers in assisting them to comprehend what is expected of them by others in summative processes. Second, marking each others' work fosters an appreciation of the need for criteria in order to make the distinction between good and not so good responses (2003, pp. 54-5).

> **Task 3.1**
> Look at the ten principles established for assessment by the *Assessment Reform Group*. How many of these are already in use in your everyday classroom practice? Could you add to this list? Are all of equal importance in your view?

## Planning a formative strategy

A baseline distinction between formative and summative assessment is that formative assessment is for the purpose of regular review of progress to inform a learning programme, while summative is for national tests and qualifications. Teachers in FE are required to know the distinction between formative and summative procedures and to apply these to a learning programme. Summative assessment is normally that which comes at the end of a course of study, usually as a formal procedure, or, in the case of a period of study over years, there may be a few such procedures which collectively produce a final mark or grade for a student. The reason why summative assessment has traditionally assumed such importance is that it has provided the basis for selection or progression. Viewed from a learning perspective, however, summative processes represent the final 'post', whereas formative assessment is a naturally occurring part of what goes on every day in the FE classroom, and provides the preparation for summative achievement. It is often informal, taking the form of questioning during individual or pair and group-work activity or observation of a student's work. More formal opportunities can occur through written work, which requires sometimes verbal, usually written, feedback. Evidence that formative assessment is taking place can come from both teachers and students. Teachers need information from formative assessment activities to inform planning and are required to reflect and evaluate such activities as part of their professional role in order to track progress and modify schemes of work where necessary to improve achievement. If, after a skill has been demonstrated in class, the practice phase shows that a significant proportion of students cannot perform the skill on their own, there will need to be a period of reflection on why this is so. It may be that the demonstration needed to be broken down into smaller stages for practice purposes, or that some students were not concentrating and so missed some of these stages. Others may not have focused very well on what was happening because they did not feel engaged in the learning. In reflecting on the activity it will be important to ascertain from the students themselves *why* they struggled. This is about learner involvement and shared responsibility in the learning and assessment process. It is also about finding the right method to assess learning, which is the focus of the following chapter. Formative assessment is often achieved through questioning processes, which are useful with both groups and individuals. Asking questions allows a teacher to test the level of understanding students bring to their learning and offers opportunities for correction. It also provides information on how challenging students are finding the learning and whether they need differentiated tasks in order to feel stretched or whether they need extra support to reach the required standards of achievement.

From a student perspective, formative assessment should help to build confidence and motivation: this is the sixth principle from the list on page 31 cited at the start of this chapter.

Sometimes, encouraging students of any age to be actively interested in assessment is a struggle! All too often learners exhibit an emotional response to feedback and results – often a defence mechanism that is being put into place as a result of previous negative experiences of assessment. This is because assessment has often been seen as a *win* or *lose* situation. These barriers can manifest themselves as anger, disappointment or indifference. Sometimes learners are shocked by their performance, perhaps because they have had unrealistic expectations. Mature adults are often, although not always, open to a dialogue with their tutor about results of assessment. Younger adults, by contrast, can be resistant to such an idea unless it is part of a planned strategy. This is where peer assessment can bridge the difficulty some students have in discussing their work with others and there is a discussion of this in Chapter 4.

Planning a formative strategy is crucial in ensuring that potential for learning is heightened. This is integral to planning for learning. Jones (2005, p. 6) points out that this process 'does not happen incidentally', and offers a series of pointers that highlight the need to plan formative assessment within an overall plan for learning:

1  Decide what is going to be learned in a particular session.
2  Define the learning goals.
3  Communicate the learning goals to the learners.
4  Compile questions and design tasks to check learner understanding of the learning goals.
5  Explain to the learners the criteria that will be used to assess their work.
6  Decide how feedback is going to be provided.
7  Decide how learners will take an active part in the assessment process.
8  Plan opportunities for learners to use the feedback provided on the assessment decision to further progress.

A good scheme of work will contain details on the first three points on this list within the aims and objectives. The remaining five refer specifically to a formative assessment strategy that needs to be planned on a lesson by lesson basis and communicated clearly to students. And part of the evaluation of the session will need to focus on how well questions and tasks worked. Such information is best recorded in note form – it is unlikely to stay in the memory!

Point 6 in Jones' list is about feedback and Chapter 7 provides guidelines for how this is given.

---

**Task 3.2**
Discuss with a colleague which areas of assessment practice you might want to revisit in order to take on board Jones' recommendations.

---

## Explaining assessment criteria

The fifth point Jones makes about planning for learning is about the clear communication of assessment criteria to students. This is often a 'missing link' between the setting of the criteria and the production of a student's work. The irony is that teachers need to assess *understanding* of these criteria before students embark on their tasks. What seems obvious to us as teachers in terms of the meaning of written criteria is by no means obvious to students. The authors have watched novice teachers explain in their own words what is meant by a set of criteria and then ask the class if they understand. There is usually a poor response! Why? Because students are either embarrassed in front of their peers to say that they do not understand or because they actually believe that they do! So an active strategy needs to be used to find out how students have interpreted criteria, usually in the form of questions. It is often the case that once one or two questions have been posed by the teacher, then the students begin asking their own. Sometimes, and this has already been mentioned in the previous chapter, the issue is to do with language. Bearing in mind that feedback should be given using, broadly speaking, the same language in which the criteria are expressed, it is worth spending time defining carefully frequently used terms that students are likely to meet in the course of their studies. Chapter 7 has a section on handling effective feedback.

## Linking formative assessment to personal development planning

The use of ILPs (individual learning plans) will also be explored in Chapter 7, where certain principles for maintaining a simple, yet effective, document are proposed. To conclude this chapter it is sufficient to say that ILPs should contain information about significant achievements along a learner's path of progress and that there is a place within them for recording formative assessment results. For if formative assessment helps learners to identify areas to focus on for improvement, then it is useful to record such information so that both student and teacher have an indication of how progress is being made and at what pace. Written records on individual feedback sheets attached to assignments have their value, but, even when work is kept in a file, it is not easy to see at a glance how well someone is doing. It is a *coherence* of information therefore which the ILP can provide, recording brief, yet significant, detail about completed assessments alongside targets set for week to week or month to month. In this way a qualitative and individual record of improvement can be maintained by staff and students alike. This will facilitate short- and long-term reviews of progress in which there has been an active commitment. The value of formative assessment does not evaporate with memory, but is utilized purposefully. It places learning at the core of the learner's experience of assessment. The research findings of Black and Wiliam, now developed to include assessment practice in all sectors of education, and not just schools, provides teachers and students alike in FE with the inspiration to make assessment a positive and worthwhile activity.

# 4: How to assess

The techniques and methods used to assess students are many and various. Within the lifelong learning sector innovative, as well as traditional, methods are encouraged in the quest to find appropriate ways of assessing the learning of a diverse student body. Professional standards for teachers and tutors in the lifelong learning sector as they relate to the assessment of students require them to select, use and evaluate assessment methods, and to use them 'fairly, effectively, equitably and consistently' to produce 'valid, reliable and sufficient evidence' (LLUK 2006). Teachers are expected to employ methods which are particularly effective in measuring learning in their own subject area. In line with the ethos of innovation, some of these assessment methods should involve the use of 'new and emerging' technologies.

A cardinal rule of assessment practice is that methods are selected for their fitness for purpose and their validity. There should also be a *variety of methods* in any strategy and a practitioner needs to distinguish between methods used as part of a formative strategy, over which there is a degree of teacher autonomy, and working with the summative methods prescribed by an external body.

Since assessment is part of curriculum planning, it must always be aligned with teaching methods. The *constructive alignment of learning outcomes to assessment methods* (Biggs 1996) is accepted as a way of ensuring that all elements of the teaching and learning process are harmonized and that subjectivity is diminished. Using constructive alignment reduces the 'convenience and preference' approach to the choice of assessment methods that can otherwise influence decision making.

The *effective use and management of methods* is essential to their success as learning tools. Effective use includes planning and managing informal classroom-based methods of assessment, such as question and answer and types of peer assessment, through to the organization of external assessments and pre- and post-assessment issues arising from the use of online assessment.

## Choosing assessment methods

Certain principles must govern the use of methods: these overarching principles were examined in some depth in Chapter 2. The methods of assessment used must be valid, reliable and practicable and must offer the student the best opportunity for achievement, which is why it is important that methods should be congruent with the overall teaching and learning strategies that students experience on a programme. If, for example, role play is a commonly used method to practise communication skills within a given subject, then it will also be appropriate as an assessment method. If, however, it is not part of ordinary classroom activity, then to introduce it as an assessment method without warning might deter some students from demonstrating their potential. In theory, finding appropriate methods seems straightforward. In fact, the application of validity, reliability and practicability to the testing of knowledge, skills and understanding is quite a complex process and this means that establishing a formative assessment strategy requires careful thought.

There are various ways of categorizing assessment methods. A starting point might be to distinguish between methods that will be used formatively and summatively, to ensure that the strategies used in everyday classroom activities assist students towards completion of summative tasks, but do not replicate them. If, for example, a student is required to write a reflective account as part of a summative submission, then formative reflective writing tasks may be an obvious choice of method. Equally, question and answer may be a relevant method of informal classroom assessment, using increasing levels of higher-order questioning to encourage the practice of 'reflective skills' requirements. As with teaching and learning, methods can also be thought of in terms of level. When planning assessment in the cognitive domain, Bloom's taxonomy of educational objectives (1956) can help teachers to determine questions which help assess how well students operate at different cognitive levels in accordance with their ability and level of study.

In the same way as it is possible to categorize teaching and learning strategies, assessment methods can also be thought of in terms of who and what they involve. These would include those involving classroom interaction (between teacher and learner or learner and learner), which might include questions, role play, games, discussion and those that are exploratory (learners working alone), examples of which are individual tasks, experiments and writing tasks (Rogers 1996, p. 142). This kind of categorization might be extended into thinking about varying and balancing an assessment strategy in terms of tasks that are individually based and those which are interactive.

---

**Task 4.1**

Consider the techniques you use in your subject area to assess your students and score them on a scale of 1 to 5, with 1 being low and 5 being high, in terms of validity, reliability and authenticity. An example is as follows.

| Technique | Validity | Reliability | Authenticity |
|---|---|---|---|
| Observation of skill (example) | 5 | 3 | 5 |
| | | | |
| | | | |
| | | | |

---

Student preference may also have a part to play in an assessment strategy. The Learning and Skills Research Centre (LSRC) research into the deployment of assessment methods in post-16 learning (Torrance 2005, p. 42) concluded: 'methods come with the "territory" of a régime, a type of qualification, a programme and a personal identity and are therefore bound up in defining qualifications' – an interesting view of the relationship between methods and courses. A crucial finding from the study was that those interviewed were largely accepting of the assessment methods used on their courses, which comprised coursework, practical assessments and tests. Attitudes to the methods themselves, as expressed by both older and younger learners in FE, were that they were appropriate. This extended perhaps unexpectedly to the use of examinations, although testing and examinations as methods had an impact in the affective domain for older learners whose memories of these from bad experiences at school were understandably negative. In a survey of the most and least popular methods, of those experienced by interviewees, the ranking was as follows:

1 written assignment (most popular)
2 online tests
3 practical tests
4 observation by assessor
5 external exam
6 project work (least popular).

Other significant findings from the report were the dislike among many adult returners of presentations, on account of the feeling of exposure, and a split opinion on exams, between those who welcomed them because they were 'out of the way' after a couple of hours, and those who felt burdened by the pressure in a short space of time. There were marked differences of opinion also between A level students, who seemed motivated by writing tasks, and NVQ students, who preferred online tests and practical work and feared writing tasks.

The report also distinguished between 'methods in action' and 'methods in principle', citing an example from research with AVCE and A level students into their reception of three methods: observation, practical tests and simulations. In this survey, observation by an assessor was deemed to be preferable (46 per cent) to simulations (26 per cent), but scored less favourably in comparison with practical tests (84 per cent). Although such statistics have to be seen against a given context, they nevertheless point to a wider issue – that of student attitude, which the report says is relevant to planning for achievement and progress in learning.

An earlier research report (Torrance 2004) presented a number of challenges for the post-16 teacher, focusing on the issue of motivation in the assessment of post-16 young adults, finding that assessment was often experienced as burdensome. One of the main findings of the 2005 LSRC report was that there is a link between motivation and learning styles and that the use of a wider range of assessment methods should be encouraged. There was disquiet within these programmes by students, teachers and assessors alike that awarding bodies set too many written tasks and too few practical assignments, and that methods did not mirror the reality of the workplace. This view concurs with that expressed in the Foster Report (Torrance 2005, point 241): 'the assessment systems are still too demanding on teacher and learner time'.

The report also warned against assessment regimes that 'dominated the learning process'. This comment on the dangers of assessment – driven learning is reminiscent of the standard attainment tests' furore in the UK in the late 1990s, which resulted in the paring down of content in the National Curriculum after criticism that too much classroom time was being absorbed by testing, with insufficient time to teach the content that was being tested! There is great value therefore in considering the variety of methods at a teacher's disposal, as opposed to 'staying safe'. Many can be discarded as unsuitable for particular subjects, but should be rejected only after they have been subjected to some scrutiny, and have been rated for their validity and reliability (Armitage et al. 2007, Ch. 6). A note of caution is sounded by Ecclestone (2003, p. 28) about choosing methods: 'strong political and social pressures pull the mindset and practices of practitioners and learners towards assessment that certificates achievement'. The pressure to meet targets, she asserts, can compromise choices about methods to use in a formative strategy which can result in formative assessment consisting of: 'the systematic accumulation of small summative assessments broken down from the demands of the qualification' (2003, p. 29). Such an approach does not accord with the concept and practice of assessment *for* learning explored in the previous chapter and does not take account of the idea that assessment should follow 'staged' learning. It is also likely to limit the repertoire of methods used, even though it is likely that there will be methods used summatively that are also used formatively.

The use of innovative assessment techniques relates mainly to those which involve online assessment. A recent Scottish Qualifications Authority (SQA) pilot project (2006) involved the use of wikis and blogs, previously used as a learning method, as part of an assessment experiment. Candidates undertaking a *Health and Safety in Care Settings* programme will produce an online presentation using a wiki, developed by SQA, for producing a collective project with discernible individual contributions. The Qualifications and Curriculum Authority website has case studies outlining various projects in UK FE colleges where ICT is being used for learning and formative assessment. SQA provide guidelines for planning and delivering computer assisted assessment (CAA), which range from the conceptual, that is, why the choice of online assessment might be made, through to the design and development of items, and also practical concerns such as the security of the material, and software and hardware concerns. Having a good rationale for using e-assessment alongside or instead of traditional methods is important. It should not be used for the sake of using technology.

---

**Task 4.2**
Did you identify any e-learning assessment tasks in the previous task, and, if so, what form did they take? Discuss with a colleague the feasibility of introducing such tasks into your assessment schedule. You will find reading about the SQA pilot useful for this exercise.

---

## Constructive alignment and assessment

The use of 'constructive alignment' is a way of ensuring that teaching, learning and assessment are congruent. The concept was created by Biggs (1996), who built on previous ideas of constructivism and reflective practice in suggesting ways of making assessment more meaningful for students. A constructivist approach to education emphasises the idea that meaningful learning itself only occurs as a result of engaging in learning activities, rather than as a result of teacher input. While developed as a mode of thinking about learning and teaching within an HE context, Biggs' ideas are relevant to any teaching and learning situation. Drawing on the idea of 'meaningful learning', Biggs urges those who design the curriculum to 'align' all parts of it in order to maximize learning, arguing that harmony among the learning and teaching strategies, the content and the assessment, will produce an ideal of 'deep learning'. If this alignment is absent, the curriculum will lack coherence and this will be to the detriment of the student. To provide this type of harmony, assessment must be fully integrated in planning the curriculum and not bolted onto a scheme of work as an afterthought.

In Biggs' system, teaching *supports* learning and the teacher has a responsibility for 'qualitative' assessment, which Biggs defines as a student's performance against the learning objectives. Criterion-referenced assessment is the form of assessment favoured with constructive alignment because it offers a measurement against such objectives, rather than against individuals. Weyers (2006, p. 71), writing about the FE curriculum, says that when using a constructivist framework the following elements are of importance:

- The learning environment, activities and assessment should encourage problem solving, critical thinking and reflection.
- Knowledge construction rather than reproduction should be emphasized in the classroom, learning activities and assessment.

Task 4.3 offers an insight into the basic principles of constructive alignment and allows a close examination of objectives and assessment criteria.

**Task 4.3**

The following questions are relevant to the principles of constructive alignment and to assessment. Take one programme you currently teach and examine the scheme of work you use against them:

1 Are the objectives linked to content and is this content relevant in all areas to the syllabus/curriculum?
2 How do the teaching and learning strategies help learners in the classroom to meet the outcomes?
3 Are the objectives linked to the criteria for assessing the programme?
4 Are the assessment methods currently being used to measure performance against these criteria valid, reliable and practicable?

## Managing an assessment strategy

Finally, the issue of managing an assessment strategy involves attention to delivery and evaluation – successful use of methods can be compromised by students not understanding what is required of them, for example. This is not a problem with the method per se, but one of communication weaknesses. Teachers should clarify the rationale for using methods with students, so that they are fully conversant with what is expected of them. In her section on the process of assessment Jones (2005, p. 22) suggests the following format for managing assessment with learners:

- brief learners on what they have to do and what they have to hand in
- introduce the assessment criteria to learners and check their understanding
- provide learners with opportunities to apply the assessment criteria to examples of work produced, possibly by a previous cohort, to illustrate standards required.

Assessment methods should also be evaluated regularly on a 'post-use' basis to check their validity and reliability in practice. An aspect of this evaluation should also be enquiry into how well the formative methods assist with summative achievement, and data from staff and students is useful for this type of analysis.

The issue of resources is also of importance in managing methods. Some assessment activities require very few resources but a lot of preparatory endeavour, such as the development of a series of 'graded' questions to develop critical skills. Multiple-choice tests can be marked quickly by either teacher or student, but are also very time-consuming to write.

Others need a lot of 'resource planning', because they involve and/or rely on equipment; such methods may also need a back-up strategy in case of equipment failure. Quizzes and games can take less preparation, but require careful classroom management to ensure fairness and in order to be able to check individual learning within a team context. Assignment/essay marking and portfolio checking require a lot of time outside the classroom, even though they are easier to set.

Key issues for awarding bodies and institutions in terms of delivering and managing online assessment are those of quality assurance and technical security and management. For this reason most awarding bodies have policies on the use of electronic assessment and it is worth checking these carefully. Part of the Introduction to Edexcel's *Policy on Electronic Assessment* (2003) reinforces the importance of sound management of electronic assessment: 'the effective use of electronic assessment will require an appropriate infrastructure to be in place to ensure that all stages of the assessment are to required standards. . . . an audit trail of such assessment will be expected to show compliance with this policy.'

In summary, it has been shown that a number of issues need to be considered when choosing and using assessment methods. These include:

- whether methods are being chosen for formative and/or summative purposes and how the two strategies 'harmonize'
- the availability of time and resources
- the alignment of methods to teaching and learning
- selecting a variety of methods that are valid, reliable and practicable

- where appropriate, the use of innovative methods such as
  e-learning.

Choosing methods is about being conscious both about the
*variety* of methods available and ensuring that they are appropriate in the ways discussed in this chapter for effective learning.

# 5: Where to assess?

Assessment in the workplace, or simulated work environment, is a requirement for NVQ, the leading vocational qualification. The *key components* of work-based assessment are universal, with examining boards basing their performance criteria on national standards drawn up by employer-led standard setting bodies. Although there are *clearly defined roles* in carrying out work-based assessment such as the assessor, supervisor, internal and external verifier, in practice, assessors may also act as supporters, tutors, trainers and the boundaries between roles can blur. There is a range of *assessment methods* which are appropriate for assessing achievement in workplace settings, each of which has particular strengths. Apart from the workplace, there are other settings which might form the basis of the assessment of FE students, all of which provide opportunities for the *assessment of activity-based, real-world experience and learning.*

## Components of work-based assessment

Each element of an NVQ unit has a set of performance criteria against which evidence for the successful completion of the element should be set. These performance criteria are sometimes presented as learning outcomes or competencies which is why evidence-based assessment is often known as 'outcome-' or 'competence-based' assessment. Unit evidence requirements then specify what the nature of the evidence should be, including the range of evidence, the detail and the assessment methods which are most appropriate. Finally, knowledge requirements will specify the key concepts and principles which underpin occupational performance as well as external factors which might affect the vocational role such as legislation and policy.

**Task 5.1**

Below are the performance criteria for Element A1.1 'Develop plans for assessing competence with candidates', in Unit A1 'Assess candidates using a range of methods' from the OCR *Learning and Development Level 3 NVQ*. What might the performance criteria be for Element A1.3 'Provide feedback and support to candidates on assessment decisions'?

You must be able to do the following:

a) develop and agree an assessment plan with candidates
b) check that all candidates understand the assessment process involved, the support available to them and the complaints and appeals procedure
c) agree fair, safe, valid and reliable assessment methods
d) identify appropriate and cost-effective opportunities for assessing performance
e) plan for using different types of evidence
f) identify how the past experience and achievements of candidates will contribute to the assessment process
g) identify and agree any special arrangements needed to make sure the assessment process is fair
h) identify how other people will contribute to assessments and what support they may need
i) identify how to protect confidentiality and agree arrangements to deal with sensitive issues
j) agree how you will handle any difficulties or disputes during the assessment
k) agree when assessment will take place with candidates and the other people involved
l) agree arrangements with candidates for reviewing their progress against the assessment plan
m) review and update assessment plans to take account of what the candidates have achieved.

## Organizing work-based assessment

Assessment which takes place in a work environment, whether it be a training workshop, simulated environment or the workplace itself, requires a particular approach and organization. Key roles in this process will be played by the assessor and the internal and external verifiers.

## The assessor

The assessor will be someone with current working knowledge and expertise in the occupation in question. They will have had experience of assessment in the work environment, will have engaged in updating their occupational knowledge and skills and will be expected to have undertaken learning and development units, depending on the role they play. They will be expected to be familiar with the occupational standards and competent to make assessment judgements using the assessment methods prescribed. They will need to plan the assessment with the candidate: the timing, the context and the evidence required. They will decide on which assessment methods to use and may help candidates to gather appropriate evidence for each. They will make the assessment decision, ensure it is accurately recorded and give the candidate feedback on their performance.

## The internal and external verifiers

Each award within a training or work organization will have an internal (IV) and external (EV) verifier. The former will be in regular contact with assessors, supporting them and monitoring their performance and the progress and achievement of candidates. Verifiers will be moderating assessment, ensuring that the standards of performance and the quality of assessment are consistent across assessors' judgements. They ensure assessment meets equal opportunities requirements and effective health and safety procedures. In addition, EVs advise and support IVs and audit the internal quality assurance processes from an external point of view. There is also a national standardization process.

---

### Task 5.2

In groups, you may all be teaching in the same curriculum area of your own or another institution. Or you may be from different curriculum areas in the same or different institutions. In each case, share your experiences of assessment and internal and external verification and consider the approach taken to each aspect of the assessor's and IV and EV role as described above.

## The role of assessors

It is rare for assessors to be involved in assessing work only. As we have seen above, even as part of the assessment task they will be supervising and supporting candidates and giving them feedback. They may need to play a variety of roles. Mentoring has become increasingly popular as a means of managing and assessing work-based learning (indeed, there are NVQ awards in workplace mentoring and coaching). Some of the roles involved in mentoring are set out in the diagram on page 52 according to whether they are directive or non-directive in nature, whether the role is passive or active and whether it is nurturing or stretching.

---

**Task 5.3**

Consider your own roles as a work-based trainer and assessor. Which of these is on the diagram and would you therefore describe yourself as directive or non-directive, active or passive, or stretching or nurturing in your approach or a mixture of the three? Are there tensions between the roles you play? Does the need to supervise and assess conflict with the nurturing, motivating and encouraging role, for example?

---

# Methods of workplace assessment

## Direct observation

Direct observation of activities carried out in the workplace allows an assessor to witness candidates' occupational skills at first hand in a 'real' situation, as they are used. The advantage is that judgements about competence can be immediate, based on the performance of the candidate at that time. On page 53 is a direct observation of a candidate in the workplace undertaking a Retailing NVQ.

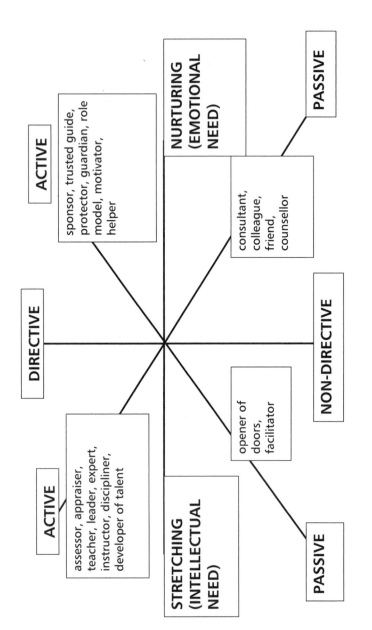

ACTIVE

sponsor, trusted guide, protector, guardian, role model, motivator, helper

NURTURING (EMOTIONAL NEED)

PASSIVE

DIRECTIVE

consultant, colleague, friend, counsellor

NON-DIRECTIVE

ACTIVE

assessor, appraiser, teacher, leader, expert, instructor, discipliner, developer of talent

opener of doors, facilitator

STRETCHING (INTELLECTUAL NEED)

PASSIVE

Adapted from Klasen and Clutterbuck (2002)

| Mid-City Training Services | |
|---|---|
| **NVQ Retailing** | Level 2 |
| **Unit** D Improving Customer Service | **Placement** Hawkins Ltd, Sheldon |
| **Element** D.1 Resolve Customer Service problems | **Date of Observation** 29.1.2007 2–3.30pm |
| **Candidate** Jim Bright | |
| **Activities Observed** | **Performance Criteria** |
| A customer brought in an MP3 player which he claimed kept malfunctioning. Jim went carefully through the operating procedure and asked the customer what had happened when the customer had tried several operations. He asked detailed questions about charging the device, for example. He then presented the options open to the customer and stated the advantages and disadvantages of each. The customer was dissatisfied with each of these and asked to see a manager. Jim complied. | D.1.3 Listen carefully to customer to understand problem raised D.1.4 Request relevant information about problem not mentioned by customer D.1.5 Be aware of realistic options to deal with complaint D.1.5 Agree an option with the customer D.1.5 Be aware of when to refer the complaint to a colleague or manager D.1.6 Work with others to manage a complaint |
| **Assessment Feedback** | |
| You handled the customer, who was angry and raised his voice, in a way which was calm and reasonable. Your questioning of the customer's actions with the device were sensible. You accurately presented the options open to the customer. Your decision to refer the complaint was well judged. | |
| **Assessor** | J. Wright |

## Witness testimony

Assessors usually visit trainees in workplaces or placements but can only make judgements about occupational skills in situ on the basis of specific visits. It is therefore useful to have the testimony of an expert witness, such as a supervisor, manager or co-worker, who is able to provide testimony which provides supplementary or supporting evidence. Brian Peacock, below, is able both to corroborate the assessor's evidence and to provide additional evidence of the same achievement at different times. Examining boards prefer expert witnesses to be familiar with the standards of the NVQ the candidate is taking. It may also be appropriate to produce service-user testimony although, as might be imagined in Jim Bright's case, accessing the evidence from the service user might not be practicable.

| Expert Witness Testimony | |
|---|---|
| **NVQ Retailing** | Level 2 |
| **Unit** D Improving Customer Service | **Placement** Hawkins Ltd, Sheldon |
| **Element** D.1 Resolve Customer Service problems | |
| **Candidate** Jim Bright | **Witness Name** Brian Peacock |
| **Witness Role** Department Manager | **Witness Signature** |
| Are you familiar with the relevant NVQ standards? | |
| On 29.1.2007 Jim Bright referred a customer to me who had brought in an MP3 player. Jim accurately and speedily conveyed to me the details of the conversation he had had with the customer. His account confirmed that he had handled the customer well and he followed company policy in referring the customer to me. Jim has demonstrated equal skill on a number of occasions when customers have been dissatisfied with services or products and has always acted according to guidance given at his induction when his placement commenced. | |

## Personal statement

The personal statement by the candidate provides an opportunity to demonstrate their knowledge and understanding with relation to occupational skills directly. Candidates can indicate their level of understanding and particularly how they have related their knowledge to practice in a way that few other methods of evidence can.

| Personal Testimony | |
|---|---|
| **NVQ Retailing** | Level 2 |
| **Unit** D Improving Customer Service | **Placement** Hawkins Ltd, Sheldon |
| **Element** D.1 Resolve Customer Service problems | |
| **Candidate** Jim Bright | **Candidate Signature** |
| **Evidence No.** | **Assessor Signature** |
| **Testimony** | **Performance Criteria** |
| I have dealt with a number of customers who have brought back items they have purchased. I have found the college assignment we completed, as well as a DTI fact sheet we were given by Hawkins at our induction, extremely useful in knowing about aspects of the law relevant to this part of my job. Although it is company policy that a manager has to authorize exchanges and refunds, my knowledge of the law is helpful in advising customers. | D.1–6 |

## Questioning

Although the assessor was able to witness directly Jim's occupational skills, there were key aspects of the knowledge and understanding relating to these skills which observation would be unable to verify. Further questioning of the candidate would be a means of testing Jim's knowledge and understanding. For example, is his product knowledge sufficient for him to advise the customer about the operation of the device? The advantage of using questioning in the workplace is its practicability in contrast to other methods of gauging knowledge and understanding such as assignments and tests. The assessor could note the key questions in advance and record the responses either in an interview schedule or audio tape them for later transcription.

## Professional discussion

It may be appropriate, usually at Level 3 and above, that questioning develops into a more detailed, two-way conversation about the occupational competencies demonstrated. Again, the focus here would be on knowledge and understanding related to the competencies and a discussion offers the opportunity for the candidate to demonstrate their understanding in greater depth about why they took the decisions to act in the particular ways that they did.

## Video/DVD/still photography

Visual evidence can be useful as additional or supplementary evidence that an assessor or other witness was unable to verify. The subjects of this visual record may be a particular work product, such as a prepared or cooked dish, or an occupational activity such as wearing appropriate protective clothing or contexts in which the candidate worked, as in the different departments of a store.

## Product evaluation

A product will be an item produced by the candidate as part of their work and will depend on the vocational area the candidate is working in. Jim Bright, for example, might have completed a refund form as a result of his exchange with the customer.

---

**Task 5.4**

Here are five assessment criteria taken from 'Preparing to Teach in the Lifelong Learning Sector', the new threshold teacher training course which began in 2007. Decide for each of these which methods of workplace assessment could be used and how you think assessment should be carried out.

1.1 Review own role and responsibilities and boundaries of own role as a teacher.

1.2 Summarize key aspects of relevant current legislative requirements and codes of practice within a specific context.

2.1 Identify, adapt and use relevant approaches to teaching and learning in relation to the specialist area.

3.1 Plan a teaching and learning session which meets the needs of individual learners.

4.4 Demonstrate good practice in giving feedback.

## Assessment in non-work contexts

Apart from the workplace, there are many other contexts in which learning and assessment can take place rather than in the classroom or training room. What such places have in common is that they offer the opportunity for the kind of practical, active, first-hand learning and assessment which is difficult to carry out effectively or to simulate in a classroom setting. Some of these contexts may be based in the FE college: laboratories, studios and workshops are examples. Other contexts may be outside in the community or beyond it. Key learning activities and events are as follows.

### Field trips

These are normally associated with particular subject or curriculum areas such as geography, geology, environmental studies, when the objects of the study are physically accessible in the environment. However, they may be relevant to subjects in the social sciences in which the focus of the field trip might be data gathering or what can be socially observed. Assessment of learning on field trips will depend on the aims and objectives the tutor sets for it. These may be focused on specialist skills associated with the subject, such as the ability to identify and gather specimens in geology. However, learning related to more generic skills such as gathering and organizing information might be assessed. External trips of all kinds provide excellent opportunities for developing and assessing key skills, particularly the wider key skills: improving own learning and performance, working with others and problem solving.

## Outdoor activities

Outdoor activities offer an ideal opportunity for a range of learning activities but particularly those relating to personal development. In addition, physical skill development and fitness, leadership skills, teamwork, planning and problem solving are areas of learning which outdoor activities can foster. Assessing learning can be problematic because personal qualities and attributes can be difficult to measure and the requirements of assessment may affect students' motivation to participate in what are usually enjoyable activities. Again, outdoor activities are ideal for developing and assessing the wider key skills.

## Community-based activities

As the FE curriculum becomes more diverse and differentiated, so the contexts in which learning and assessment take place need to be broader. The community can act as a resource for learning activities relating to both academic and vocational subjects: a survey of shoppers' views and habits might form the basis of work in GCSE business studies or NVQ business administration. The local community may act as a focus for work in subjects such as citizenship for example. It is perhaps most used as a context for learning in programmes which have personal effectiveness and personal and social development as key aims. Learning will often take place in projects in which students might engage with the community in a variety of ways, from a support and caring role with the elderly to peer mentoring of younger students. ASDAN (Award Scheme Development and Accreditation Network) awards and those of the Duke of Edinburgh's Award Scheme are typical of those which would consider community-based activities as central to student achievement.

## Educational visits

Many FE colleges charge students a fee for visits which arise as part of their programme. Potential venues for such visits are limitless but will include visits to art galleries, museums, sites of historical interest, theatrical performances, holiday resorts and leisure centres, manufacturing, shopping centres, newspapers, broadcasters, sports events, hotels, farms, hospitals, police stations, and fire and rescue stations. Learning on educational visits is necessarily experiential and activity based and appropriate assessment strategies will be those which can be used on-site, such as task sheets which involve students following a route through the venue exposing them to the information and experience the tutor requires, or completed soon after the experience, such as a play review. Photographic and film records of the visit can be used as a part of the assessment task after the event.

---

**Task 5.5**

In the table below is a series of active learning experiences and assessment strategies. Decide which assessment strategy(-ies) would be most appropriate for each active learning experience. Where this was difficult, what more did you need to know about the learning experience to help you?

| Active learning strategies | Assessment strategies |
|---|---|
| • Land-based outdoor activities: pot-holing, abseiling, canoeing<br>• 'When I was Young': GCSE history students research the 1940s by interviewing elderly people in a drop-in centre<br>• Art and design students studying window display – visit to a shopping mall<br>• Planning and preparing an information evening for school students applying to FE<br>• GCE A/AS computing students visit Bletchley Park National Codes Centre (www.bletchley park.org.uk) | • Observation<br>• Peer assessment<br>• Diary<br>• Short answer worksheets<br>• Descriptive record of the visit<br>• Critical account of visit<br>• Photographs<br>• Video record<br>• Self-assessment<br>• Display/group or individual presentation<br>• Audio record<br>• Design and make a product<br>• Drawing<br>• Interview record/transcript<br>• Others? |

- Child care students mount a poster exhibition 'Children Playing'
- Public services students camp overnight supervised by army personnel who teach camping, fieldcraft and survival skills
- GCE A/AS theatre studies students visit the theatre
- A/AS art: textiles students visit the Victoria and Albert Museum (www.vam.ac.uk)
- A/AS history students visit the Victoria and Albert Museum

**Task 5.6**

Either alone or in subject/curriculum area groups, devise an active learning session in either a work or non-work context and specify how you would assess student achievement.

# 6: Who assesses?

Assessment practice nowadays involves a range of people: tutors, adults other than tutors, such as workplace supervisors and learning assistants, 'unseen' examiners from boards and, of course, students themselves. Just *who* really assesses in post-compulsory education is a key question, possibly with a rather depressing response! Race (2005, p. 81) claims that 'each assessment judgement is almost always initially made in the mind of one assessor in the first instance', even though that judgement is often mediated by others.

*Self-assessment* has in recent years become a widespread practice, as seen in Chapter 2, and is supported by educationists on account of its benefit as a learning tool. It is important to determine its appropriateness within programmes however, and in the 'Self-assessment' section below the 'when' and 'how' of self-assessment are examined.

*Peer assessment* has become increasingly popular as a practice and also brings with it both strengths and weaknesses as a tool. The benefits and issues are similar to those in self-assessment, but factors of *reliability* and *management* also prevail, as will be seen in the section 'Peer assessment'. In 'Assessing students outside the classroom', the responsibilities of those adults who assess students outside the classroom are examined, with a focus on the need for clear communication channels between all those involved in the assessment process. There is now an increased emphasis on the quality control of assessment at all levels and Ofsted in England and Estyn in Wales have assumed a prominent role in this process. 'Quality-assuring assessment' will consider how the quality of assessment is controlled through the following mechanisms: the institution, moderation, and internal and external verification. This section will also explore who is responsible for establishing assessment criteria and the rise in the role of the chartered assessor.

---

**Task 6.1**

Before reading the remainder of this chapter make a list of those who hold responsibility for assessment processes in your establishment. This will include not only those who design the assessment strategy, but also those who assist with its delivery, such as examinations officers. How do you in your role relate to those you have listed?

---

## Self-assessment

Historically, only teachers and those 'external' to an educational establishment carried out assessment. Nowadays the practice of self-assessment is widespread and is viewed as a valuable learning tool for students. This is because self-assessment involves *reflective* practice, in which students have to evaluate their own performance and are therefore, it is argued, more likely to be actively involved in the assessment process. From this follows an opportunity to develop evaluative skills which will ultimately assist in improving performance. The way in which self-assessment can enhance the quality of a student's performance is well documented. Many findings came out of the study by Black and Wiliam (1998), examined in Chapter 3, and their innovative research in helping students to assess their own performance. Their ideas on the inclusion of the learner in assessment through self-activities and peer activities spring from the constructivist approach to learning described in Chapter 4, in which 'learning and assessment processes and activities are rooted in particular forms of co-operation and social inter-action' (Ecclestone 2003, p. 88). In this approach, using self-assessment and peer assessment makes it easier for learners to *construct* an understanding of the 'gap' between current and desired performance and to work out strategies of how to move from the former to the latter. Self-assessment therefore has an important role to play in the practice of assessment for learning first explored in Chapter 3.

Issues of appropriateness must be determined in planning to

include self-assessment as part of an overall assessment strategy. It is likely that an attempt to use formative assessment will provide many opportunities for reflection on assessment tasks and the skills, knowledge and understanding tested through these. If a self-assessment strategy is to be successful, the students will need to be taught the skills to carry out such measurements of their performance, whether it is of a vocational or academic nature, and also to see this type of assessment as an activity with status. In a sense the two go hand in hand. Teaching students these skills is valuable, as they will be able to transfer them from one context to another. It is here that links between self-assessment and peer assessment can be drawn, on the basis that part of the skill of self-assessment can be learned through seeing the work of others. It has been pointed out that it is easier to pinpoint the deficiencies in others' work than in one's own (Jones 2005, p. 20). It might therefore be pragmatic to introduce peer assessment first and then encourage learners to bring to the assessment process realistic expectations about summative performance, removing some of the mystique associated with an assessment regime in which only tutors or outsiders measure performance. It stands to reason therefore that there must be careful management by teachers of any self-assessment process in order for students to establish realistic expectations of themselves.

It should also be clear that some students will struggle with the process, since the development of evaluative and critical skills is challenging for many. For some, depending on age and previous experience of learning, the whole notion of self-assessment and peer assessment may be problematic and may be perceived to lack validity. After all, this is a new phenomenon, which challenges long-held views about only teachers or external examiners and assessors possessing sufficient knowledge, experience and, of course, power to make judgements about student work.

If self-assessment is part of a continuous formative assessment process, integral to the everyday learning experience and bringing clear results, then it will be seen as valuable.

If the value is not seen, then students are more likely to feel that only their teachers should be assessing them!

**Task 6.2**

How would you explain the benefits of self-assessment to your students? You will need to think about their age, the level of the programme they are taking and their ability, as well as examples you could offer them.

## Peer assessment

Peer assessment is related to self-assessment and is a practice that is also becoming more widespread. While self-assessment involves a two-way dialogue between learner and teacher, peer assessment can be more complex, involving the tutor in checking and monitoring the validity and reliability of the process. For bias can easily distort peers' views of each other's work, interfering with the co-operative and collaborative conditions which underpin constructivism. Students must be encouraged to objectivize their assessment of others in the same way as their teachers, through applying assessment criteria rigorously. In order to do this, they must first prove that they can understand and use these criteria in a context outside of their peers, that is, on the work of (anonymous) previous students where possible. They will need feedback on how well they are doing in developing skills for this.

Second, a teacher's management skills may be important in determining who peer assesses whom, if known tensions between groups and individuals in the class exist. Younger learners in particular sometimes find it hard to put aside dislikes and work non-competitively with their peers.

Clearly, helping students to develop such skills and monitoring peer assessment and self-assessment requires time and patience, often at a premium in the FE setting. The skills are taught, not picked up. Yet Black and Wiliam (1998, cited in Armitage et al. 2007, Ch. 6) state that formative assessment of this type generates evidence used to adapt the teaching work to meet the needs of learners, and so is at the heart of a learner-centred approach.

It may be the case that what is still a fairly radical approach to assessment practice requires a re-organization of time above all. In addition to time, skilful management of these two types of assessment is vital if they are to be embedded properly in everyday practice. This involves not only monitoring issues of validity, reliability and suitability but effecting long-lasting attitudinal beliefs in who may assess. These will only take root if students can see tangible rewards in their learning.

## Assessing students outside the classroom

It is common for many students in FE to be assessed by a range of people, with and through the assistance of adults other than their tutors. These divide into those who work in the same organization as the tutor and those who work outside. Examples of those working inside and outside the FE setting include workplace supervisors for students on vocational programmes, those who support students on a regular basis in the classroom, such as assistants, and those who are employed on a temporary basis to assist students with varying disabilities who require support to complete (often) summative assessment processes. One of the key issues in workplace supervision is that of the importance of communication between the FE college and the place of work. Problems and communication breakdown can arise when the criteria and competencies have not been sufficiently well explained to workplace supervisors, as a result of which the student may feel that although they are the *focus* of the assessment process they are in receipt of conflicting advice and information about what is expected of them. This can jeopardize their assessment performance and is a situation over which they have little control and is thus disempowering. Workplace mentors and supervisors need not only access to relevant documentation such as unit specifications, but also a mechanism for collaborating with course tutors to ensure that there is a shared understanding and interpretation of such documentation and of what is required from workplace assessment.

**Task 6.3**

A good way of ensuring that those in the workplace are aware of their responsibilities and feel supported by the college tutors is to outline these responsibilities in a letter. What would be the key information you would need to relate in such a letter?

## Quality-assuring assessment

As with educational processes generally, there has been a pro-liferation of quality-assurance mechanisms in the UK PCET sector throughout the last decade. These range from internal to external, from procedures for measuring assessment results at institutional level through to external moderation and veri-fication controls.

A recent development in the trend towards refining assess-ment has been the creation of the Institute of Educational Assessors – a chartered, independent professional body of educational assessors set up in 2006, whose role is to provide support, advice and professional development for teachers wishing to develop assessment skills. The Institute also has the declared aim of establishing greater public confidence in stan-dards, publicizing goals of introducing mark schemes which are: 'externally and independently audited by chartered assessors belonging to the Institute' (www.ioea.org.uk). It is in the area of formative assessment that the Institute envisages its profes-sional development role. The mission statement strongly sup-ports the notion of the 'assessment community' of the UK, comprising every person involved in assessment practice – internally or externally. At the same time as promoting a sense of inclusion, however, it also lays down the idea of 'qualifying' to assess and introduces another layer in the hierarchy of assessment practitioners.

**Task 6.4**

Look at the Institute of Educational Assessors' website at www.ioea.org.uk. What benefits do you think it might bring to you personally in your professional capacity?

It has been pointed out that there is a distinction between quality 'control' and quality 'assurance' (Ecclestone 2003, p. 40). Both are key procedures in this discussion of 'who' assesses. Within *quality control* there are those who:

- approve the running of curricula and programmes in centres against centrally designed and evaluated criteria
- develop tests and material for both
- develop guidance for carrying out assessments
- carry out internal moderations of results and internal verification of assessment procedures.

Those included under the umbrella of *quality assurance* are:

- external moderators from award and lead bodies
- those who verify the activities of external moderators
- those who determine 'best practice' awards for quality assessment and control mechanisms (Ecclestone 2003, p. 40–1).

Gaining a good knowledge and understanding of quality control and assurance processes takes time, but it is essential for working effectively with students to help them maximize achievement. A full explanation of how the institution assures quality assessment and the responsibilities of individual tutors in respect of internal and external verification and moderation should be a mandatory part of a teacher's induction in a college. Sadly, this is often not the case, making inexperienced teachers' understanding of such processes partial. This can in turn undermine their explanations of how assessment works with their own students and can lead to problems of confidence.

On a more optimistic note, staff development opportunities for learning about assessment have improved in recent years in most colleges. New teachers should ask for clear definitions and explanations of processes and procedures: the new professional standards for teachers and tutors in the lifelong learning sector (www.lifelonglearninguk.org) stipulate that a teacher should understand the procedures for conducting and recording internal and external assessments. The standards also require teachers to work 'as part of a team to establish equitable assessment processes', a philosophy endorsed by the Learning and Skills Development Agency (LSDA) (Jones 2005, p. 9) to 'encourage team involvement in defining any strategies designed to promote change, whether it be imposed by external agencies or within an institution'.

The quality of information available to teachers about processes and especially summative procedures is also greatly enhanced nowadays by the internet sites created by bodies such as QCA (www.qca.org.uk) whose code of practice quality assures the setting and management of assessment procedures and whose website offers clear guidance for practitioners. An explanation of the 'examination process', for example, is also available on the Edexcel website (www.edexcel.org.uk), showing in diagrammatic form the 'life cycle' of an examination. The overview also explains how various committees' reviews and meetings handle and determine standards and grades and use data to compare individual institutions' results within previous programmes. It defines the various categories of personnel in terms of title and role: examiners, assistant examiners and moderators. Information on the edexcel website about examination processes explains how the many employees from edexcel seek to ensure validity and reliability at national level. Such websites should be consulted frequently for up-to-date information about assessment issues.

---

**Task 6.5**

Make a list of issues which you are unclear about in relation to the summative assessment processes you are involved in with your students. Then look at the websites of the examination boards relevant to the qualifications you teach to see how many answers you can find.

---

In considering 'who' is involved in the assessment process it is useful to draw the distinction between formative and summative assessment. Teachers are of course involved in both processes. In formative assessment they are largely autonomous within their teaching teams, to make their own decisions about how best to use assessment *for* learning, which will almost certainly include the strategies of peer assessment and self-assessment. Their involvement in summative assessment processes brings them in touch with external assessment bodies and agencies, whose focus is on the quality control and assurance of examinations and awards; these bodies are themselves quality kitemarked by QCA, and are often large and complex organizations.

In summary, many people have a hand in student assessment, from the students themselves, their teachers and the institutions they operate in, through to external bodies and those who quality assure them. To this end the assessment process is of interest to all, but the teacher is pivotal within the entire process. To survive in FE a teacher must therefore be clear about their roles and responsibilities in this process and he/she has a right to high-quality information and professional development to help them undertake such a role. Thinking beyond the individual responsibilities of all those who have some involvement in the assessment process, however, a closing thought from Race (2005, p. 81) alerts us to the need for collective action in changing what it is that we perhaps do not like about the current national assessment system:

'Living on a crowded planet may be a collaborative game, but we tend to play the assessment game in predominantly singular circumstances, and competitive ones at that. The fact of the matter is that to fix assessment in post-compulsory education will require individuals to change what they do, but that won't be enough to change the culture. Teams of individuals with a shared realization of the problem will need to be the first step.'

# 7: Recording and reporting achievement

As we saw in Chapters 1 and 3, one of the principal aims of assessment is the giving of formative *feedback* to students to enable them to learn more effectively. Feedback can be given to students in a variety of ways. Written feedback is arguably the most widely used in FE but oral feedback is gaining increasing importance, particularly in tutorial sessions in which learning is reviewed and targets set for students. In many programmes, blended learning will lead to the giving of e-feedback on work submitted online and which might take place through a virtual learning environment. The *monitoring and recording of individual progress* and achievement is now a standard process in FE, usually linked to the completion of an individual learning plan or progress development plan. It is also common practice for tutors to engage in more at-a-glance *record keeping*, which enables them to read off student progress more easily. Summative *reporting of achievement* will take place at the end of a module or course. The nature of such reporting will depend on the referencing type of any assessment being reported, the intended audience or end-user – taking into consideration the need to balance the report's content and currency,

## Feedback

Effective feedback should be:

*Specific* There are two ways in which feedback needs to be specific. First, although there is a place for generalizations which pick out key features of the work overall, comments which refer to particular parts or points, even sentences and phrases of written work, are more likely to enable students to act upon them. A rule of thumb for written summative comments is not to make a comment unless you can point to clear evidence to substantiate it in the body of the work. Second, it is very tempting when marking a number of assignments to concentrate on features common to them all. Try to tailor your comments to all the relevant features of individual pieces of work which relate to the assessment criteria.

*Timely*   As a rule, feedback should be given as soon as practicable after the assessed work has been completed. The longer the gap between the two events, the more difficult it is for students to relate the feedback to their work. Students also, rightly, interpret the length of time between completion and feedback as a judgement by you of the value of their work. Lengthy turnaround times can also weaken the effect of positive feedback to students.

*Comprehensible*   It is a common occurrence when work is returned to students that, after the immediate silent concentrated reading of the feedback sheet, the hands go up and they ask, 'What did you mean by this?' Brief, unexplained words or phrases in the body of the work such as 'Sale of Goods Act?' 'Germany' 'and what else?' will only need unpacking and explaining so it is worth being clear and explicit in writing in the first place. In addition, feedback needs to be written in a language you know your students are going to understand. Torrance (2005) vividly illustrate how students struggle enough with the language used by awarding bodies for competence-based assessment programmes before even beginning to interpret tutor comments.

*Developmental*   One of the key reasons for giving feedback is for students to learn more effectively and develop the quality of their work. Feedback therefore needs to let them know what they did well and why. And it should help them do what they did not do as well, better. It will only be formative if you are constructive and suggest ways in which they might do this.

*Motivating*   Feedback is one of the most important vehicles for motivating learners. And negative or inadequate feedback is an enormously powerful factor in de-motivating them. Indeed, research has indicated that students who withdraw from their FE courses are more likely to claim they did not get sufficient feedback on their assignments than those who continue (Martinez and Munday 1998).

*Personalized* It is tempting to adopt a formal tone when giving feedback on the grounds that this will give the commentary a measure of both authority and objectivity. However, a more friendly conversational tone in which you address the student by name will give them the impression that the feedback is addressed to them as individuals.

*Practicable/Realistic* Feedback should take the ability and developmental stage in learning of the student on the programme into account. It should suggest ways of improving work which the student might reasonably be expected to be able to achieve.

*Structured* Tutors sometimes write feedback in no particular order, as it occurs to them, without considering the student's need to interpret and assimilate it. It is much more helpful to students when it has a structure and the main points have a logical sequence. This may be working from the beginning of the work to the end, numbering points in the body of the work and dealing with each in turn on the assignment sheet. Alternatively, the sequence may be to cover the main categories of assessment, or the extent to which key learning outcomes or assessment criteria are met.

---

**Task 7.1**
Below is an assignment mark sheet. To what extent do you think the tutor's feedback exemplifies the features of effective feedback described above?

---

| Spurlington College | | | |
|---|---|---|---|
| Assignment Mark Sheet | | | |
| **Name** | Jermaine Green | **Course** | AS Psychology |
| **Group** | 2 | **Unit** | Individual Differences |
| **Submitted** | 16.3.07 | | |

As noted in previous assignments, it would be a good idea to have an introductory paragraph which sets out your intentions. It would have been better to have begun looking at key concepts of the learning approach rather than plunging into specific experiments. Overall, you demonstrate an understanding of the distinction between classical and operant conditioning but there is some confusion: the acquisition of social skills is an example of operant rather than classical conditioning. Your accounts of Pavlov's and Skinner's experiments are comprehensive and accurate and illustrate well the distinctions between these two kinds of conditioning. However, you might have supplemented these with reference to other experiments such as those of Bandura, for example, on observational learning of aggression. I did feel your reference to both psychodynamic and physiological approaches did not help with your main task in the assignment which was to describe the key features of the learning approach and this section felt like padding. You must work at your written style – there are too many grammatical inaccuracies here including ellipsis, disagreement between pronoun and verb as well as errors of punctuation including incorrect use of the apostrophe and comma. You need to read more widely than the main text in future and if you simply quote sources without indicating how they illustrate your discussion, the assessor cannot be certain you understand them.

**Tutor** ... L. Watson ........................ Date. . .20.4.07 ........................

# Recording and monitoring individual progress

Ofsted have identified the quality of progress reviews as a frequent weakness in inspection reports, the key weaknesses being inadequate progress reviews, weak target-setting for learners and slow progress by learners, which is not being identified and tackled through the progress review process.

---

**Task 7.2**

On the next page is a tutorial record sheet for Jermaine Green. How far does it demonstrate target-setting that is SMART – Specific, Measurable, Achievable, Realistic and Timely? Consider the progress review process for your own students. What are its strengths and weaknesses?

---

| **Spurlington College** |
| :---: |
| **Tutorial Record Sheet** |

**Name:** Jermaine Green
**Course:** AS Sociology, Psychology, Media Studies, Art, English
**Date of Meeting:** 7.4.2007

**Progress against previous learning targets:**
1. Meeting assignment deadlines – Assignment deadlines in psychology, sociology and media studies have been met since half term, although Jermaine is still behind in art and English assignments.
2. Reading – Jermaine still needs to read more widely, particularly in psychology and sociology.
3. Note-taking – this has improved immensely – Jermaine has used well the techniques we discussed at the last tutorial.
4. Essay structure – this has improved but there still needs to be more thought on Jermaine's part about his overall organizational approach.
5. Participation in class activities – Jermaine has still been a passenger in class activities rather than an active participant.
6. Written style – reduce grammatical inaccuracy and errors of punctuation in written work.

**New learning targets:**
1. Meeting assignment deadlines – Jermaine to draw up a timetable/completion programme for organizing his assignment writing.
2. Reading – Jermaine to consult with tutors and draw up a list of reading for each assignment.
3. Essay structure – Jermaine to include essay plans with each assignment.
4. Jermaine to demonstrate more active participation in class activities.
5. Jermaine to proofread his work and ask others to do this.

**Summary of tutor/student discussion:**
Jermaine appears better motivated in sociology, psychology and media studies than in art and English as evidenced in the variation in his completion of work. He agrees that is true and ascribes it to his not continuing with these two subjects in his A levels next year. Jermaine has done little thinking about what subject/s he wishes to study at

university and indeed whether he wants to go. It emerged that Jermaine is keen to become a sports journalist and wondered whether university would further these career aims. Jermaine was referred to Student Advice and Guidance on this matter but was advised to conduct his own research on the nature of undergraduate journalism courses.

**Signature Tutor:**
**Signature Student:**

# Record keeping

If the key records of an individual student's progress are the ILP entries together with tutorial record sheets, these are likely to be kept in the student's file and may be difficult and time-consuming for tutors to access. Even if photocopies are kept of tutorial record sheets and assignment mark sheets, it is useful for tutors to keep more at-a-glance records which enable them to read off student progress more easily. This also allows tutors to compare aspects of an individual student's progress and achievement with that of others in the group. If work is handed in late by individual students, this is likely to point to an individual problem, but if a significant proportion of the group is late with work then this may indicate that the course structure or assessment regime needs reviewing. Most FE colleges require tutors to write a group profile at the beginning of a course. This is helpful to other colleagues who may share teaching or make an occasional input, as well as inspectors and other observers, but it could be conceived of as the initial profile of individuals which then continues as a set of individual records throughout the course. Such records are useful to feed into progress reviews or tutorials as well as summative reporting of a student's achievement at the end of the course or year. There is no best practice recommendation for the form such records should take and individual colleges and awarding bodies may have a preferred model or template you are required to follow.

However, the content of the record might include:

- comment on attendance and punctuality

- a record of assessment tasks, submission dates and a summary of achievement
- comment on behaviour and attitude to work
- any significant achievement in class-based work or tasks not formally assessed.

The record should ideally be:

- depending on the intended currency of the record, comprehensible to relevant third parties
- easy to keep
- simple, with a limited amount of information
- easy to read in tabular or diagrammatic form.

There is a range of software available which not only allows records to be made electronically but also integrates course and lesson planning with record keeping. One software program enables stakeholders such as parents to access tutors' records online.

---

**Task 7.3**
Share any individual records you keep of your students' progress. Compare them with respect to the content and ideal features described above.

---

## Reporting on achievement

Whereas the feedback and reporting in the previous sections of this chapter is formative in nature, there is a need for reporting on achievement summatively, either at the end of a unit or module or at the end of a course or programme.

---

**Task 7.4**
As you complete this task, consider what implications it has for your writing of reports on your students' achievements. If in a group situation, select a member of the group and, in no more than half a page, describe them. Take it in turns to read out your descriptions to the rest of the group. Then consider the questions below:

- How quickly did they recognize the subject?

- What aspects of an individual were included in the portrayal – physical characteristics, aspects of personality, clothing, personal attributes?
- Was the subject described clearly?
- Did the lack of a specific purpose for the portrayal (such as for the college's marketing for example) make it difficult to complete?
- How far did the portrayal rely on the portrayer's or the group's previous knowledge of the individual? Do you think outsiders would have recognized the subject from the description, for example?
- Did the knowledge that the portrayal would be read out affect its construction?

The aspects of a particular set of achievements selected for any report will be determined by the referencing approach taken for the assessment which produced them. We looked in detail at referencing approaches in Chapter 2 and, although there is use of unreferenced open portrayals, graded scale and criterion referencing are the most prevalent underpinning reporting practices in FE.

Criterion referencing assumes a series of criteria against which achievement is judged. But there are many ways in which that judgement can be made and presented. The criteria against which Jim Bright's achievement below is being assessed are performance criteria. And the judgement amounts to a series of 'can do' statements or competencies, evidence for which Jim has demonstrated.

| Mid-City Training Services | |
|---|---|
| **NVQ Retailing** | Level 2 |
| **Unit** D Improving Customer Service | **Placement** Hawkins Ltd, Sheldon |
| **Element** D.1 Resolve Customer Service problems | **Date of Observation** 29.1.2007 2–3.30pm |
| **Candidate** Jim Bright | |

| Activities Observed | Performance Criteria |
|---|---|
| A customer brought in an MP3 player which he claimed kept malfunctioning. Jim went carefully through the operating procedure and asked the customer what had happened when the customer had tried several operations. He asked detailed questions about charging the device, for example. He then presented the options open to the customer and stated the advantages and disadvantages of each. The customer was dissatisfied with each of these and asked to see a manager. Jim complied. | D.1.3 Listen carefully to customer to understand problem raised<br>D.1.4 Request relevant information about problem not mentioned by customer<br>D.1.5 Be aware of realistic options to deal with complaint<br>D.1.5 Agree an option with the customer<br>D.1.5 Be aware of when to refer the complaint to a colleague or manager<br>D.1.6 Work with others to manage a complaint |
| **Assessment Feedback** | |
| You handled the customer, who was angry and raised his voice, in a way which was calm and reasonable. Your questioning of the customer's actions with the device were sensible. You accurately presented the options open to the customer. Your decision to refer the complaint was well judged. | |

However, 'can do' statements tell us very little about the quality and standard of Jim's achievement. And a graded scale, 1–10, A–E, of itself, would tell us even less. But assessment schemes which attempt to associate levels of achievement with grades or points on a scale, might tell us more.

| Unit D Improving Customer Service | | | |
|---|---|---|---|
| **Listening** | Limited attention paid to customer complaint | Pays attention to complaint but does not have full understanding of it | Listens carefully and checks understanding of complaint |
| | | | ✓ |
| **Elicits information** | Elicits limited information from customer | Elicits information from customer but not all is relevant | Gains all information relevant to complaint |
| | | | ✓ |
| **Management of complaint** | Loses control of exchange or antagonizes customer further | Addresses complaint but some mishandling or mis-understanding | Calmly and reasonably deals with customer |
| | | | ✓ |
| **Product knowledge** | Product knowledge insufficient to diagnose problem | Product knowledge sound but not applied fully to problem | Thorough application of product knowledge which leads to likely diagnosis of problem |
| | | | ✓ |
| **Presentation of options** | Not all options clearly presented | Options presented but no advice on recommended course of action | Options clearly presented with advice on recommended course of action |
| | | | ✓ |

From the above, it can be seen that the strengths of using grade descriptors are:

- they are clear, accessible, easy to read
- they show progression in learning
- they indicate a level of achievement.

However, limitations include:

- a tendency for descriptors to jump, not demonstrating the even progression of achievement their presentation implies
- not describing individual achievement distinctly.

# 8: Assessment in society

The increased emphasis on assessment within the learning and skills sector is widely accepted in day-to-day practice. It is part of a trend throughout the UK education system to measure and formalize achievement of candidates – a trend which can be questioned in terms of its wider implications for society. This chapter investigates the question of the wider implications of current UK assessment processes for society. For society at large, of course, 'assessment' is synonymous with qualifications, and it is qualifications that have been at the centre of much controversy in the lifelong learning sector in recent years.

*Credentialism* – the growth in the importance of certification and qualifications – has consequences for students, teachers and their employers and is a trend which derives from a particular ideology about the status of qualifications in society. The *'standards' debate* continues to attract the interest of employers, politicians and educationists, providing a variance of opinion about falling and rising levels of achievement, who controls them and their implications for UK education in a competitive global market. Linked to the standards debate is the use of *qualifications as performance indicators* and *the role of inspection processes* in defining levels of performance – two often contentious areas of assessment practice. Finally, the use of *assessment for selection* purposes determines the manner in which society values achievement and raises questions about the criteria guiding such important decision-making processes.

## Credentialism

The concept of credentialism has arisen from the creation of a 'knowledge economy' in the Western world and is linked to another dominant ideology: the 'learning society'. In a knowledge economy it is technology-led businesses, predominantly IT focused, that are presented as the main generators of knowledge that contribute to a country's economy. The role played by 'knowledge' in this type of economy shapes the value placed on certain types of qualifications and thus distinguishes 'achievers' from 'non-achievers' within such a framework. As Race comments, our society rewards students 'for what they *show*, not just for what they know', creating a situation where the latter is almost more important than the former. 'In some assessment contexts', he writes, 'learners can gain credit by becoming competent at writing as if they had mastered something, even when they have not' (Race 2005, p. 68).

Guile (2003) attributes the idea of credentialism, that is, the importance attached to qualifications, within a learning society and knowledge economy, to government-led educational policy which views the former as essential to employment. This is linked in turn to 'supporting national prosperity' (2003, p. 92). The ideology of the knowledge economy is reflected in the links between qualifications and their application to industry. One of the aims of the new specialized diploma, for example, is to provide industry-verified applied learning, linked to general learning, which has credibility within UK industry (www.qca.org.uk).

The triangle of qualifications, employment and economic success can be traced back, arguably, to Callaghan's famed speech in the Great Debate of 1976, but, as Guile observes, in the new millennium it does not take account of emerging 'social and political problems that cannot merely be resolved either through managing access to, or by varying the delivery of, the same type of education and training' (2003, p. 93).

Politicians have tried through recent decades to justify an increased emphasis on educational achievement and qualifications also in terms of their importance for global competitiveness and have looked primarily at vocational education and training and higher education to fulfil these aspirations. Several writers have countered such arguments by comparing the UK to other nations in such terms, pointing out (Tomlinson 2001,

p. 207) that in maths and science tests pupils from Bulgaria and the Slovak Republic performed well without any significant economic advantage to those countries, while the United States had lower scores but was economically strong.

Wolf (2002) endorses such views, challenging what she believes to be the myth about education delivering economic growth by citing examples of countries that function well economically without the emphasis on training that has become one of the major obsessions of education policy in the UK in the last decade.

A further dimension to the qualifications debate focuses on the long-term use and relevance of accumulating qualifications in a society where future employment trends are more uncertain then ever before. This, of course, is also linked to globalization and the advent of the knowledge economy. There are widespread predictions of future employees needing to manage a portfolio of jobs and retrain throughout their lives to meet the imperatives of a changing economy and workplace. This reality poses some threat to the enduring certainty of qualifications in enabling the securing of long-term employment. Despite such uncertainties, industrialists contribute vociferously to the national debate on the subjects that young people should be studying and to the issue of why some subjects appear to be falling from favour. In 2005, for example, the CBI expressed its concern over the unpopularity of modern languages, maths and science by comparison with the high numbers of students opting for media studies and psychology (MacLeod 2005). This pronouncement unleashed criticism on the assessment of the former subjects, with claims that getting good A level grades in the first three is more difficult than in psychology and media studies, thus putting assessment centre stage as a reason for their unpopularity.

This type of debate adds to challenges faced by practitioners in the FE sector, who have to defend the importance of qualifications to those they teach while preparing young people for the rapidly changing world of employment in which the currencies of qualification inevitably date quickly.

This challenge of preparing young people for an uncertain world of work is also rendered more complex by constant curricular reform, triggered by Curriculum 2000 at the beginning of the millennium and characterized presently by the introduction of the specialized diploma. The latter qualifications continue the aims of Curriculum 2000, to develop social learning (Lea et al. 2003, p. 42) and to help young people 'combine practical skill development with theoretical and technical understanding and knowledge' (www.qca.org.uk). One consequence of such complexity is the ever-increasing need for professional development qualifications for staff to support students in FE and community learning. In short, credentialism does not only affect students but it also extends to their teachers as well! This can be readily confirmed by looking at the LLUK website (www.lifelonglearninguk.org), which each year publicizes a plethora of new specialist qualifications for staff in the post-16 sector.

The emphasis on the acquisition of qualifications has led to an instrumentalist attitude on the part of many students and institutions towards assessment. This is unsurprising, given the pressure on providers to ensure the success of their students. A recent LSRC report (Torrance 2005) notes that when interviewing students in FE about progress and achievement, the ability to articulate personal achievement in terms other than those linked to award and certification was uncommon. This will be the long-standing legacy of credentialism.

## The standards debate

The worth of qualifications is linked to the standards debate, which began in earnest in the compulsory sector with the Education Reform Act of 1988, which made schools more accountable for their results and introduced market forces into the educational arena. Its effects have spread very powerfully into the FE sector over the last 15 years, beginning effectively with incorporation in 1993, pitting not only FE institutions against each other in terms of attracting students, but also with sixth forms in schools and sixth form colleges. In the case of A level courses, taught in all three settings, the competition for students is often keen and results, in the public domain, are perused carefully to assist in parental and student decision making.

The Nuffield Review of Learning, as part of its ongoing report on 14–19 learning in Britain, reported on a 'standards' issue in relation to preparedness for entry to university in terms of reading, communication and thinking skills. 'Negative comments are not indicative of higher education tutors and admissions staff whingeing or harking back to some golden age, but represent genuine concerns about young people and their capacity to benefit from the higher education experience' (BBC News 2006).

Not surprisingly the findings of the report were seized on by the media as a way of confirming established views about falling standards among 14 to 19 year olds. An editorial headline on the findings of the Nuffield Review (Lightfoot 2006a) read: 'Spoon-fed pupils can't cope at college'. The article exposes the opinion of various stakeholders on the issue of standards, including university admissions tutors, the CBI and academics. Blame is apportioned to two factors: those which are beyond the control of education, such as increased exposure to the internet, which has resulted in fewer books being read, and the other is the government's changes to A level which have encouraged a 'bite-sized chunk' approach to learning and the need to spoon-feed students to obtain good results for schools.

There is a consensus, it seems, that the assessment-driven regime that has dominated the pre- and post-16 education scene during the last two decades has created a greater emphasis on the need for qualifications, but, in the eyes of many, at the expense of deep learning.

Are standards rising or falling? The *Guardian* concludes that this is a 'circular argument that will never be resolved' (MacLeod 2005), for as examination boards claim vigorously that A level examinations are not getting easier, their opponents point to the increasing numbers of young people obtaining top grades as clear evidence to the contrary.

The government attributes the rise in standards to better teaching and improved sixth form colleges. MacLeod's article reported a defence of the increased pass rate in A levels to 'the background of teaching getting better. Inefficient small sixth forms have gone and now we've got cracking sixth-form colleges. I would expect a rising level of achievement'. Later that week, Wragg (2005) cautioned against a definitive stance on whether standards are rising or falling, arguing that there was insufficient data to prove anything about standards, remarking on the fact that examination boards were 'secret places'. The factors that suggest that the improvements had taken place, he argued, were threefold: the endeavour of the pupils themselves, the hard work of their teachers and the rise in the exam 'industry'. The failure of the examination bodies to allow external researchers into their realms blocked any definitive answer on the issue of falling or rising standards in his opinion: 'The question "what is happiness?", he said, could be asked of a seven-year-old, a sixteen-year-old or a final-year undergraduate philosophy student. It is what they reply and how their answer is marked that counts, and we will never know, while the exam boards remain the secret places they have always been.'

In a MORI poll of 2002, commissioned by the QCA to examine public perceptions of examinations, increased pass rates in both GCSE and A level were attributed to student effort by 41 per cent of parents and to improved teaching by 28 per cent of teachers. In the same poll, however, neither students nor teachers had a clear view over whether qualifications had greater or lesser value than in the past – an interesting observation – although there was a consensus that they were necessary for a 'good' career.

The standards debate is at the forefront of education debate at government level. While the left and right argue about the achievements of young people, they would do well to remember the disempowering experience of the system that this inevitably creates among the 14–19 population, their teachers and parents. Concerns have been expressed about this by an eminent figure. The issue of 'driving up' standards that has led to constant testing of children and young people was criticized by Archbishop Rowan Williams in an interview about the Children's Society (BBC Radio 4 2006). In the interview the Archbishop spoke of the unnecessary amount of examinations and testing, which he described as 'relentless'. It made the 'whole of the education institution anxiety driven', he commented, and he linked his views to a negative pressure on young people to another concern, namely the distinct fear of failure: 'when you surround educational institutions with criteria hoops to jump through, if you put it a bit crudely, then of course there's going to be some element of fear, and some element of fear that somehow your professional skills are not taken seriously'. Despite such soundings it seems unlikely that the current fixation with standards will dwindle. The Leitch Review of 2006 has suggested to the government that in order to even keep pace with global competitors, the numbers of UK citizens with qualifications will need to increase substantially over the next decade; Gordon Brown has spoken on several occasions since taking office of the importance of the FE sector in achieving this.

---

**Task 8.1**

The tasks in this chapter are discussion points The first discussion point is whether standards in the subject area(s) you teach have risen, fallen or stayed the same, in your opinion? What evidence could you produce to substantiate your views?

---

## Qualifications as performance indicators

The establishment of league tables across all sectors of the education system in the UK arose out of the concept of accountability. FE is no exception in this regime of inspections and league tables. While a need for accountability of some description is largely uncontentious among most practitioners, the way in which it operates is the subject of much disquiet. In addition to the usual criticisms of burdensome bureaucracy in preparation for an inspection itself and subjective reporting on the part of inspectors, there is widespread anecdotal evidence of a lack of confidence in most FE staffrooms about the usefulness of inspections in improving standards. In particular, there are concerns about the distortion of 'value-added' in FE colleges that the use of an over-simplistic scoring system can create. Many colleges are dealing with 'mixed-economy' students, that is, those taking both academic and vocational qualifications, as well as catering for a very broad spectrum of young and older adults taking an equally broad range of qualifications. Since retention is a principal goal within the ethos of FE institutions, corresponding to the notion of 'finding the right course for the right student', movement across courses within an institution is widespread and might itself be regarded as an internal indicator of achievement. In terms of performance tables, however, this is an invisible 'value-added' phenomenon. Second, the scoring system is also said to distort achievement, on account of the fact that certain qualifications do not count towards the accumulation of points on which scores are based. Third, there is, and has been for some years, criticism from FE colleges that they are compared unfairly with schools who select the better students at age 16. Against these misgivings about performance indicators from the sector are media reports of improved success rates in certain areas of performance, such as the LSC's report (2007) about 'record success rates' for 2005/6, with a percentage claim of 77 out of 100 students in FE across the country achieving a qualification in the course they studied for, surpassing the target set for them by the government. This 'success' story is linked to the economic well-being examined in the first part of this chapter: 'We have reached our interim target of one million adults achieving their first full level 2 qualification . . . and this is good news for the economy', says the report.

## Assessment and selection

One of the commonly recognized purposes of assessment is its use in selection processes. Chapter 1 focuses on initial assessment in determining the suitability of students for particular courses in further education. Selection processes are also used to help students make choices about progressing onto other courses within FE, onto higher education or into employment. Selection and progression issues are complex and varied within post-16 education.

Progression cannot just be viewed in terms of the accumulation of certificates in preparation for further study and/or occupation – it is a far more complex phenomenon. Definitions of progress can be divided into those that are *vertical* – moving up the qualifications ladder – and *horizontal* – an aggregatory acquisition of modules at the same level of difficulty (Torrance 2005, pp. 28–9). So, for example, an FE student might be studying NVQ Level 2 and AVCE modules concurrently. Can this be regarded as progression? Nowadays, students are also gathering credits of parallel worth across different subjects, such as Basic Skills and GCSEs. Progression for some students can also constitute movement from academic into vocational routes and then, in later life and perhaps still within FE, back into academic pathways. For those who have struggled on academic routes, 'progression' occurs at a point where they are able to achieve in the vocational arena; in short, progression is, to some degree, in the eyes of the individual.

---

**Task 8.2**
Should we foster an attitude that everyone can progress in education, or is there a limit to what some students can achieve? What is your opinion on this, based on your experience?

---

Rates of progression are also important to FE establishments in terms of funding, and to politicians, who will draw an equation between standards and progression. Critics of the insatiable quest for qualifications will suggest that the obsession with progression as part of the lifelong learning agenda is about massaging employment statistics and bringing educational policy into the labour market.

Progression is presented to FE students as a prerequisite for economic well-being, although this message might be regarded as largely ineffectual in a system where financial incentives such as the Education Maintenance Allowance are necessary inducements to keep certain young people in full-time education.

Selection for higher education has been the source of controversy in the last few years for different reasons. One of these is the controversy that has had to do with social engineering. The government has attempted in the last few years to encourage students from disadvantaged backgrounds to enter university, taking account of the effect of social and economic factors on academic achievement – a move which has led to accusations of social engineering. Recent statistics, however, suggest that such policies have been ineffectual in altering the domination of university places by the middle classes. Despite Labour's campaign in the last five years to encourage a higher proportion of working-class children to seek university places, there has been an actual decline in applications from this group. Research (Lightfoot 2006b) has reported the highest drop-out rates from less economically advantaged backgrounds and those with low A level scores. These participation rates have been a disappointment to all concerned, and strike at the heart of a deeper debate about the nexus between social class, aspiration and education. Furthermore, some universities have complained about the way in which HESA has used overly complex formulae established by a 'performance indicators steering group' to make judgements about their falling short of targets for admitting students from poorer backgrounds (BBC News 2004).

Another contributing factor among students from poorer backgrounds in certain areas of the UK may be the steady decline in the manufacturing industries linked to an instrumentalist view of young people that qualifications were a 'currency that could be exchanged for work opportunities' (Tomlinson 2001, p. 208). If the latter are removed, as they have been so often in the last few years, the currency understandably loses value.

The Schwarz Review (DfES 2004a) made a number of recommendations of relevance to the problem of selection for HE, one of which was in relation to this issue. It suggested that it was not the responsibility of higher education to make up for educational or social disadvantage. It will be interesting over the next decade to see how government policy with regard to attracting greater numbers from economically disadvantaged backgrounds develops.

Another source of assessment and selection controversy is the introduction of university admission tests to differentiate between the brightest A level candidates. This move has arisen largely from the discrediting of A levels in terms of their predictability of good students for certain courses. The Tomlinson Report (Working Group on 14–19 Reform 2004) suggested that some universities were experiencing difficulty in selecting the brightest students and this is unsurprising in a system in which 20 per cent of A level candidates in 2004 were awarded an 'A' grade. As a consequence, research is underway to develop a system for a 'scholastic aptitude test', along US lines, with the progress of young people currently undergoing a 'SAT' trial through A level and subsequent degree being monitored over a five-year period to assess the suitability of the test as a predictor of achievement. A university entrance test of this kind is seen as a potential method for widening participation by its supporters and as yet another divisive move to advantage the middle classes by others.

It is clear that assessment issues outside the classroom are as complex and problematic as inside! Debates about qualifications, progression and selection lie at the centre of individual social and economic well-being, social cohesion and national and international standing. The assessment regime for young people in the UK is characterized by an uncertainty and upheaval hitherto not experienced and is highly politicized. The issues explored in this chapter are likely to remain at the forefront of political and educational debate for a long time.

# 9: Frameworks and futures – assessment and qualification reform

The history of the major developments in *assessment and qualification reform* over the last 20 years is traced in an illustration of the key points underpinning current and future 14–19 and adult learning reforms. These reforms have the potential to create a standardized, unitized *credit framework* across the sector. Developments in *electronic assessment* are considered as the area in which most future innovation in assessment is likely to occur.

## Qualifications and reform

A number of key issues have been at the centre of qualification and assessment reform over the last 20 years in the FE sector:

- integration
- breadth
- depth
- entitlement
- coherence
- flexibility
- progression
- relevance.

The Technical and Vocational Education Initiative of the 1980s and 1990s introduced a series of features which promised to enhance existing qualifications. It proposed a core skills curriculum to which all young people would be entitled. It called for qualifications to have much greater vocational relevance and prepare students more effectively for the world of work. This would be achieved partly by enhancing the curriculum offer with integrated and contextualized qualifications such as design technology, media studies, business studies and electronics. It advocated the centrality of technology, ICT in particular. It introduced much wider learning contexts and the development of enterprise skills. It advocated curriculum enrichment with the development of personal and social education and careers and guidance education, for example. And finally, it introduced modularity as the basis of curriculum design.

These reforms suffered a setback in 1988 with the introduction of the National Curriculum, which prescribed a secondary curriculum made up of essentially traditional academic subjects. Reinforced by Key Stage testing, this led to a one-size-fits-all academic offer and, with the introduction of National Vocational Qualifications, the division between academic and vocational qualifications deepened and led to what Hodgson and Spours have called a 'national two-track qualifications system' (2003, p. 11). The introduction of GNVQ meant that we had a triple-track system of academic, general vocational and vocational qualifications. However, among the Dearing Report's key findings (Dearing 1996) were that the academic/vocational divide inhibited progress, there were high non-completion rates, there were levels of concern about basic literacy/numeracy skills and the qualification system was over-complex. Dearing's report led directly to the Curriculum 2000 reforms, the underlying themes of which were: broadening study at advanced level; greater consistency of standards between and within different types of qualifications; rationalizing subject specifications at advanced level; and improving alignment between general and general vocational qualifications. C2000 introduced a modular AS/A and vocational A level framework, intended to add breadth and depth as well as to maximize choice and flexibility. However, at the time of writing, we are seven years on from these reforms and the following concerns have emerged. There are consistent worries about grade inflation and the role of AS retakes in relation to this. Key Skills have been problematic to implement, either signposted in qualifications or delivered discretely. The promised breadth offered by AS levels was limited by the resource available for delivery and the complexity of time-tabling. There are concerns about over assessment and in practice the integration of AS/A and vocational AVCE/GNVQ units has had limited success.

October 2004 saw the publication of the Tomlinson Report (Working Group on 14–19 Reform 2004). Its headline features were: a multi-level system of diplomas; entry to advanced diploma 'lines' rather than an academic/vocational divide; holistic programmes of learning recognized by diplomas; a common core of learning including a personalized extended project; links with apprenticeship and work-based learning; assessment for learning; and a long-term reform process involving all stakeholders. The government rejected many of Tomlinson's recommendations and responded in the 2005 white paper *14–19 Education and Skills* (DfES 2005) which proposed: a strong foundation at Key Stage 3; a strong core 14–19 routes to success for all; a new system of specialized diplomas; strengthening GCSEs and A levels; engaging all young people; and a system configured around young people.

The specialized diplomas represent the key elements of these reforms. They will be available at levels 1–3 and the 14 diploma lines will be introduced over three years: society, health and development, engineering, ICT and creative and media, construction and the built environment from 2008; land-based and environmental, manufacturing, hair and beauty, business, administration and finance, hospitality and catering from 2009; and, from 2010, public services, sport and leisure, retail, travel and tourism. The diploma will comprise the following elements:

- Principal learning which will develop knowledge, skills and understanding in a vocational context.
- Generic learning skills which will include:
  - functional skills in English, ICT and maths at Levels 1, 2 and 3
  - six transferable personal, learning and thinking skills (PLTS) in independent enquiry, creative thinking,

reflective learning, team working, self-managing and effective participation
- a diploma project or extended study involving investigative and project management skills
- skills gained through work experience.
- Additional/specialist learning allowing students to specialize further or to select units that will complement their programme.

New criteria for GCSE are currently subject to consultation but the key concerns of the regulators are to:

- 'update the content of the GCSEs
- encourage innovative teaching, learning and assessment
- incorporate key elements of 14–19 curriculum developments
- ensure that the revised GCSEs complement the new diplomas
- revise the assessment arrangements to provide stretch and challenge for all learners and make assessment less formulaic and predictable
- ensure that standards are maintained.'

(www.qca.org.uk/qca_11693.aspx)

At the same time, revised A levels will be available for first teaching in September 2008. Changes to them include:

- 'fewer units of study
- fewer structured questions, and more open-ended questions which require extended essay responses
- more questions which require a synoptic overview of the subject
- the introduction of an extended project
- the introduction of a new A$^\star$ grade which recognizes very high achievement.'

(www.qca.org.uk/qca_13027.aspx)

**Task 9.1**
Consider the qualifications you currently prepare students for. How would you evaluate them in so far as they:

- effectively integrate content from different academic subject areas or vocational contexts
- offer breadth of learning
- offer depth of learning
- deliver a core entitlement of learning
- have a coherent structure themselves and in relation to other qualifications
- offer flexibility to the learner
- are relevant to young people's experience?

## Qualification and credit frameworks

All qualifications accredited by the Qualifications and Curriculum Authority are currently awarded at one of eight levels in the National Qualifications Framework (NQF) (see below). The NQF was revised in 2004 and aligned with the Framework for Higher Education Qualifications. Qualifications at the same level will make broadly similar demands on the learner but may vary in terms of content and length.

| National Qualifications Framework | | Framework for Higher Education Qualifications |
|---|---|---|
| *Previous levels and examples* | *Current levels and examples* | |
| 5<br>Level 5 NVQ in Construction Management<br>Level 5 Diploma in Translation | 8<br>Specialist awards | D (doctoral)<br>Doctorates |
| | 7<br>Level 7 Diploma in Translation | M (masters)<br>Masters degrees, postgraduate certificates and diplomas |
| 4<br>Level 4 NVQ in Advice and Guidance | 6<br>Level 6 National Diploma in Professional | H (honours)<br>Bachelor degrees, graduate certificates and diplomas |

| | Production Skills | H (honours) Bachelor degrees, graduate certificates and diplomas |
|---|---|---|
| Level 4 National Diploma in Professional Production Skills<br>Level 4 BTEC Higher National Diploma in 3D Design<br>Level 4 Certificate in Early Years | 5<br>Level 5 BTEC Higher National Diploma in 3D Design | I (intermediate) Diplomas of higher education and further education, foundation degrees and higher national diplomas |
| | 4<br>Level 4 Certificate in Early Years | C (certificate) Certificates of higher education |
| 3<br>Level 3 Certificate in Small Animal Care<br>Level 3 NVQ in Aeronautical Engineering<br>A levels | | |
| 2<br>Level 2 Diploma for Beauty Specialists<br>Level 2 NVQ in Agricultural Crop Production<br>GCSEs Grades A*–C | | |
| 1<br>Level 1 Certificate in Motor Vehicle Studies<br>Level 1 NVQ in Bakery<br>GCSEs Grades D–G | | |

| | |
|---|---|
| Entry<br>Entry Level<br>Certificate in Adult<br>Literacy | |

Levels 1–3 remain the same in the revised framework
(www.qca.org.uk/libraryAssets/media/qca-06-2298-nqf-web.pdf)

---

**Task 9.2**

Below are the generic level descriptors for Entry Level and Levels 1, 2 and 3, the levels at which most FE qualifications are. However, the level of each set of descriptors is not shown. With courses you teach on in mind, indicate what you think is the level of each set of descriptors. (Answers on page 104.)

---

| Level | Intellectual Skills and Attributes | Processes | Accountability |
|---|---|---|---|
| ? | Apply knowledge with underpinning comprehension in a number of areas<br><br>Make comparisons<br><br>Interpret available information<br><br>Demonstrate a range of skills | Choose from a range of procedures performed in a number of contexts, some of which may be non-routine. Co-ordinate with others | Undertake directed activity with a degree of autonomy<br><br>Achieve outcomes with time constraints<br><br>Accept increased responsibility for quantity and quality of output subject to internal quality checking |
| ? | Employ recall and demonstrate elementary comprehension in a narrow range of areas with | Operate mainly in closely defined and highly structured contexts | Carry out directed activity under close supervision<br><br>Rely entirely on |

| | | | |
|---|---|---|---|
| | dependency on ideas of others<br><br>Exercise basic skills<br><br>Receive and pass on information | Carry out processes that are repetitive and predictable<br><br>Undertake the performance of clearly defined tasks<br><br>Assume a limited range of roles | external monitoring of output and quality |
| ? | Employ a narrow range of applied knowledge and basic comprehension<br><br>Demonstrate a narrow range of skills<br><br>Apply known solutions to familiar problems<br><br>Present and record information from readily available sources | Show basic competence in a limited range of predictable and structured contexts<br><br>Utilize a clear choice of routine responses<br><br>Co-operate with others | Exercise a very limited degree of discretion and judgement about possible actions<br><br>Carry restricted responsibility for quantity and quality of output<br><br>Operate under direct supervision and quality control |
| ? | Apply knowledge and skills in a range of complex activities, demonstrating comprehension of relevant theories<br><br>Access and evaluate | Operate in a variety of familiar contexts using a range of technical or learning skills<br><br>Select from a considerable choice of procedures | Engage in self-directed activity with guidance/ evaluation<br><br>Accept responsibility for quantity and quality of output |

| information independently | Give presentations to an audience | Accept limited responsibility for the quantity and quality of the output of others |
|---|---|---|
| Analyse information and make reasoned judgements | | |
| Employ a range of responses to well-defined but often unfamiliar or unpredictable problems | | |

The consideration of qualification reform and frameworks so far has focused on those relating to young people's learning because this book is primarily aimed at those working in FE, which is now predominantly a young person's sector. However, as Hodgson et al. point out:

'Throughout the period from the late 1980s to 2003, it is possible to trace the influence of two distinct broad, but related, strands of thinking on curriculum and qualifications reform: one based on a more baccalaureate or "grouped award" approach with a focus on curriculum, coherent programmes of study and the needs of younger learners; the other emphasising an "open", flexible and unitized framework aiming mainly at the needs of adult learners.'

(Hodgson et al. 2006, p. 9)

Hodgson et al. make a strong case for the merging of these approaches in a unitized credit system. The QCA is currently piloting a Qualifications and Credit Framework (formerly known as the Framework for Achievement or FfA). All units within the QCF will be given a level and credit value. One credit is awarded for those learning outcomes achievable in ten hours of learning time. Once the unit has been developed, it is submitted to the QCF data bank. Units are then combined to create qualifications using rules of combination. Regulators accredit these qualifications when they are satisfied that they are of high quality. Once they have completed a unit, learners are awarded the relevant credits and this is recorded on their learner achievement record (LAR), an electronic record which lists an individual's credit and qualification achievements.

QCA regards the benefits to learners of the QCF as

- '[offering] learners more freedom, choice and flexibility.
- They can choose to complete units or whole qualifications.
- They can easily access information about the commitment needed for different routes to achievement, letting them balance that commitment with family, work and other responsibilities.
- They can build up credits at their own pace and combine them in a way that will help them get where they want to be.
- They can transfer credits between qualifications to avoid having to repeat their learning.
- They will have all achievements recorded on an electronic learner achievement record (LAR), encouraging them and others to value their past achievements.
- The LAR also shows learners how the credit they already have can contribute to different routes to achievement.

Benefits for learning providers (schools, colleges, workplaces) are that:

- The QCF will enable providers to design more flexible programmes, suitable to the individual needs of learners.
- The QCF can help them improve retention and progression rates by recognizing smaller steps of achievement more frequently.
- The QCF will track all learners' achievements through the use of a unique learner number (ULN) and an individual's electronic learner achievement record (LAR), giving providers standard information about each learner's past achievements.
- The QCF will help learning providers describe

achievements to employers and learners in a language that is easy to understand.

Benefits for employers are:

- The QCF will provide a quick, easy way to quantify the level and size of achievements of prospective employees.
- The QCF will give employers a way to get in-house training approved within a national framework, helping employees gain credit for achievements on employer-led programmes.
- The QCF will give employers an accessible language with which to describe and understand levels of achievements.
- Employers will be able to search online to find units that could support training for employees.

Benefits for others are:

- The QCF will provide clear information on units and qualifications on offer in England, Wales and Northern Ireland.
- The QCF will allow achievements to be transferred across national and international boundaries.
- The QCF will be an inclusive framework, containing a wide range of qualifications.'

(www.qca.org.uk/libraryAssets/media/QCF_Leaflet_final_web.pdf)

## E-assessment

In an era when Britons are the most active web users in Europe, spending an average 36 minutes online every day, when three-quarters of 11 year olds have their own TV, games console and mobile, and two-thirds of children do not believe they could live easily without a mobile and the internet (Allen 2007), it would be unsurprising if electronic assessment did not play an increasingly wider role at all levels in education including FE.

### Word processing

Perhaps the most widely used form of electronic assessment is that of word-processed text, either as hard copy or as an attachment which can be marked and annotated as a draft on-screen and combined with an e-tutorial online or via mobile phone. This accelerates the assessment process. However, the number of such drafts allowed and the nature of feedback given should be clarified to avoid the danger of 'spoon-feeding' students or of giving excessive support to more demanding ones.

## Evidence of achievement

E-assessment allows students to submit evidence of achievement which can be an alternative to text and more appropriate to the nature of the subject and the tasks being assessed. A PowerPoint presentation may demonstrate specific presentational skills. Still photographs, video or audio clips are more appropriate for achievement demonstrated outside a conventional classroom environment.

## On-screen assessment

Assessment online or using specialized software can take a variety of forms. Multiple choice tests can be completed quickly with rapid results feedback. These can be seen to be only testing superficial knowledge of a factual nature and it has been argued that all online testing will be of this kind because of the limitations on student response and online assessment of this. However, software is increasingly capable of dealing with more complex responses involving greater interactivity such as text matching, ranking, pull down lists and drag and drop. The Hot Potatoes program (available at http://web.uvic.ca/hrd/hotpot/ #downloads) allows teachers to devise tests and quizzes using jumbled sentences, crosswords, gap filling, matching, short text answers and multiple choice.

## Awarding body assessment

Awarding bodies are now extensively using e-assessment. In the summer of 2007, for example, the Assessment and Qualifications Alliance used new technology to mark nearly five million exam papers: 1.7 million of these exam papers were marked directly from a scanned image. Over 11,000 of their examiners were involved in electronic marking and mark capture, which was nearly half the total number of examiners marking their GCE and GCSE scripts. Nearly 350 exam components were marked using the full range of new technology, and GCE components were included for the first time. (www.aqa.org.uk/over/electronic.php)

## Virtual learning environments

VLEs offer the opportunities for assessor, self-assessment and peer assessment most effectively through online discussion groups. However, a range of stimuli and resources can be used to instigate, illustrate and complement these discussions, such as case studies, controversial extracts and key problems.

## E-portfolios

E-portfolios can act as or support personal development planners or individual learning plans. Students can record aspects of their learning in a range of forms, often in diary form as a log book which acts as a blog or web log. The contents of the e-portfolio can be accessed by others, particularly tutors who are able to give feedback on what has been recorded. Students can self-assess by cross-referencing their entries to learning outcomes, skills or course objectives. A range of evidence can be stored and presented in an e-portfolio, such as still photographs, audio or video clips.

---

**Task 9.3**

Consider the e-assessment you currently use. Would it benefit the assessment of your students' work were you able to use it more extensively? Are there barriers to the use of e-assessment and do these relate to you and your students, the organization you work in, factors outside your organization?

---

Level Descriptors for Task 9.2: Level 2, Entry Level, Level 1, Level 3

# 10: Summary – assessment in FE

Chapter 1 takes an overview of assessment in FE, addressing the role and purpose of assessment in the sector and begins by considering how assessment is playing an increasingly important role in the selection and admission of FE students. This is partly a result of colleges' realization in practice of what research has established – that students on the wrong course are more likely to withdraw and that thorough and searching admissions procedures will have more effect on retention. Accurate and thorough diagnostic assessment therefore has an important role to play. The key purpose of formative assessment is the giving of feedback to students for a variety of reasons: the assessment itself can be a means of learning; students are able to monitor and improve their learning; feedback, if effectively given, can motivate students and can reinforce learning. The importance of assessment *for* learning, as opposed to *of* learning, has been given prominence in recent policy initiatives, and curricular and qualifications reform. One of the issues Curriculum 2000, the Tomlinson proposals and the government's current 14–19 strategy have attempted to address is the fragmented nature of the post-14 curriculum and the absence of clear progression pathways for students. The Qualifications and Curriculum Authority is currently developing a Qualifications and Credit Framework and it remains to be seen whether this can help to clarify and simplify the incoherence of progression pathways. The assessment of vocational achievement has for the last 20 years been largely evidence based with National Vocational Qualifications and similar awards central to measuring such achievement at five levels. In addition, a second track of more general vocational qualifications, such as GNVQ, Vocational GCSE, AVCE and, from 2005, Applied GCE AS and A, will be supplemented from 2008 onwards by 14 vocational diploma lines. At the time of writing, the future relation between GCE and specialized diplomas remains unclear. The introduction of the QCF may lead to progression which is credit- as well as level-related and allow more opportunities for horizontal (across career or academic/vocational boundaries) as well as vertical progression, from one level to another.

Chapter 2 looks at *what* to assess. This involves a consideration of what can be called a framework for assessment and how assessment relates to the aims and objectives established for a particular learning experience, either through lesson plans, schemes of work, syllabuses or award body specifications. It is essential to have a referencing system for any assessment exercise and thus decisions have to be made about the appropriateness of comparisons and whether they are to be made with the performance of other students (norm referencing), against set criteria (criterion referenced) or self-referencing (ipsative assessment). One of the most important principles in assessment practice is that of validity. An exploration of this principle focuses on how validity in assessment processes is ensured, that is, how the methods used to assess learning really do measure whatever they are supposed to measure and no more or no less. Once again, this can be related back to the objectives or learning outcomes, where content, process and product – often a blend of all three – are being assessed. Another important principle in framing the organization of an assessment strategy is that of practicability – the capacity to carry out the most suitable form of assessment in the circumstances which are provided, since the inability to do this can jeopardize a well-designed assessment framework. Linked to this is authenticity – the issue of whether a sufficiently real context for assessing performance can be achieved through the tasks chosen for assessment purposes.

How can fairness in assessment be assured? Equality in assessment is an ever increasingly important issue. The growth in individualized learning presents a challenge in differentiated assessment, combined with a need to guarantee that assessors are not influenced by class, gender or cultural factors in their roles. Reliability in the assessment process increases the potential for all students to benefit from a framework which is maximized in terms of its reliability through specific performance criteria, rigorous marking schemes and sound modification and verification processes.

The central concerns of Chapter 3 are the purposes and uses of assessment as a learning experience for students. This is known as 'assessment for learning'. Chapter 1 established the importance in general terms of the process of assessment in affecting motivation and underlined the function of assessment as a guide for progression. Chapter 3 focuses more specifically on the way in which assessment should be harnessed to motivation through providing feedback on student work that allows that learner to make progress. The phrase 'for learning' may seem obvious. Until recent years, however, there has been an emphasis on the assessment 'of' learning, that is, on summative achievement, which has often been at the expense of the formative assessment process that helps the learner to progress towards these summative goals. The groundbreaking work of Paul Black, referred to in Chapter 1, and which has been largely responsible for focusing greater attention on assessment for learning throughout UK education, is examined as well as the differences between formative and summative assessment and the need to plan a formative assessment strategy. The communication of clear assessment criteria to students is considered before an examination of the role of assessment feedback in personal development planning for its contribution to student learning.

The concept of assessment for learning has been promoted vigorously by major educational groups in the last few years and in 2002 the *Assessment Reform Group* established ten principles to underpin classroom practice They are as follows:

1 Assessment for learning should be part of effective planning of teaching and learning.
2 It should focus on how students learn.
3 It should be recognized as central to classroom practice.
4 Assessment for learning should be regarded as a key professional skill for teachers.

5 This process should be sensitive and constructive on account of its emotional impact.

6 Assessment should take account of the importance of learner motivation.

7 It should promote commitment to learning goals and create a shared understanding of the criteria by which they are assessed.

8 Learners should receive constructive feedback about how to improve.

9 Assessment for learning develops learners' capacity for self-assessment so that they can become reflective and self-managing.

10 Assessment for learning should recognize the full range of achievements of all learners.

Many of these principles are implicit in the practice promoted throughout this book, but they are looked at specifically in greater detail in this chapter.

Chapter 4 considers the many and various techniques and methods used to assess students. Within the lifelong learning sector, innovative, as well as traditional, methods are encouraged in the quest to find appropriate ways of assessing the learning of a diverse student body. Professional standards for teachers and tutors in the lifelong learning sector as they relate to the assessment of students require them to select, use and evaluate assessment methods, and to use them 'fairly, effectively, equitably and consistently', to produce 'valid, reliable and sufficient evidence' (New Overarching Professional Standards, LLUK, Jan 2006). Teachers are expected to employ methods which are particularly effective in measuring learning in their own subject area. In line with the ethos of innovation, some of these assessment methods should involve the use of 'new and emerging' technologies. A cardinal rule of assessment practice is that methods are selected for their fitness for purpose and their validity. There should also be a variety of methods in any strategy and a practitioner needs to distinguish between methods used as part of a formative strategy, over which there is a degree of teacher autonomy, and working with the summative methods prescribed by an external body. Since assessment is part of curriculum planning, it must always be aligned with teaching methods. The constructive alignment of learning outcomes to assessment methods is accepted as a way of ensuring that all elements of the teaching and learning process are harmonized and that subjectivity is diminished. Using constructive alignment reduces the 'convenience and pre-ference' approach to the choice of assessment methods that can otherwise influence decision making.

The effective use and management of methods is essential to their success as learning tools. Effective use includes planning and managing informal classroom-based methods of assessment, such as question and answer and types of peer assessment, through to the organization of external assessments and pre- and post-assessment issues arising from the use of online assessment.

Chapter 5 considers the contexts in which assessment takes place and, on the basis that the key context for the assessment of FE students outside the traditional classroom is the workplace, or simulated work environment, most of the chapter is focused on the assessment of work-based or work-related learning. The key components of work-based assessment are universal, with examining boards basing their performance criteria on national standards drawn up by employer-led standard setting bodies. Unit evidence requirements then specify what the nature of the evidence should be and knowledge requirements will specify the key concepts and principles which underpin occupational performance as well as external factors which might affect the vocational role such as legislation and policy. Assessment which takes place in a work environment, whether it be a training workshop, simulated environment or workplace itself, requires a particular approach and organization.

Although there are clearly defined roles in carrying out work-based assessment such as the assessor, supervisor, internal and external verifier, in practice, assessors may also act as sup-porters, tutors, trainers and the boundaries between roles can blur. There is a range of assessment methods which are appropriate for assessing achievement in workplace settings, each of which has particular strengths. These include direct observation, witness testimony, personal statements, questioning, professional discussion, video/DVD/still photo-graphy and product evaluation. Apart from the workplace, there are other settings which might form the basis of the assessment of FE students, all of which provide opportunities for the assessment of activity-based, real-world experience and learning, such as field trips, outdoor activities, community-based activities and educational visits.

Chapter 6 observes that assessment practice nowadays involves a range of people: tutors, adults other than tutors, such as workplace supervisors and learning assistants, 'unseen' examiners from boards, and, of course, students themselves. Just *who* really assesses in post-compulsory education is a key question, possibly with a rather depressing response. Race (2005, p. 81) claims that 'each assessment judgement is almost always initially made in the mind of one assessor in the first instance', even though that judgement is often mediated by others. Self-assessment has in recent years become a widespread practice, as seen in Chapter 2, and is supported by educationists on account of its benefit as a learning tool. It is important to determine its appropriateness within programmes however, and the 'when' and 'how' of self-assessment are therefore examined. Peer assessment has also become increasingly popular as a practice and brings with it both strengths and weaknesses as a tool. The benefits and issues are similar to those in self-assessment, but factors of reliability and management also pre-vail. The responsibilities of those adults who assess students outside the classroom are examined, with a focus on the need for clear communication channels between all those involved in the assessment process. There is now an increased emphasis on the quality control of assessment at all levels and Ofsted in England and Estyn in Wales have assumed a prominent role in this process. There is a consideration of how the quality of assessment is controlled through the following mechanisms: the institution, moderation, and internal and external verification. This section also explores who is responsible for establishing assessment criteria and the rise in the role of the chartered assessor.

Chapter 7 considers how we record achievement and how we report it to students themselves and third parties such as other teachers, employers, HE institutions and parents. As was seen in Chapters 1 and 3, one of the principal aims of assessment is the giving of formative feedback to students to enable them to learn more effectively. Feedback can be given to students in a variety of ways. Written feedback is arguably the most widely used in FE but oral feedback is gaining increasing importance, particularly in tutorial sessions in which learning is reviewed and targets set for students. In many programmes, blended learning will lead to the giving of e-feedback on work submitted online and which might take place through a virtual learning environment. Feedback should be specific both in its reference to particular parts of a piece of work and in its addressing the individual achievements of a learner. As a rule, feedback should be given as soon as practicable after the assessed work has been completed. Feedback should be accessible and comprehensible to the learner and written in a language they can understand. It should be developmental in so far as it lets students know what they did well and why. Feedback is one of the most important vehicles for motivating learners and negative or inadequate feedback is an enormously powerful factor in de-motivating them. A friendly conversational tone in which students are addressed by name will give them the impression that the feedback is personalized and addressed to them as individuals. It should suggest ways of improving work which the student might reasonably be expected to be able to achieve. It is helpful to students when feedback has a structure and the main points have a logical sequence. The monitoring and recording of individual progress and achievement is now a standard process in FE, usually linked to the completion of an individual learning plan or progress development plan. Summative reporting of achievement will take place at the end of a module or course. The nature of such reporting will depend on the referencing type of any assessment being reported, the intended audience or end-user – taking into consideration the need to balance the report's content and currency.

The increased emphasis on assessment within the learning and skills sector is widely accepted in day-to-day practice. It is part of a trend throughout the UK education system to measure and formalize achievement of candidates – a trend which can be questioned in terms of its wider implications for society. Chapter 8 investigates the question of the wider implications of current UK assessment processes for society. For society at large, of course, 'assessment' is synonymous with qualifications, and it is qualifications that have been at the centre of much controversy in the lifelong learning sector in recent years. Credentialism – the growth in the importance of certification and qualifications – has consequences for students, teachers and their employers and is a trend which derives from a particular ideology about the status of qualifications in society. The 'standards' debate continues to attract the interest of employers, politicians and educationists, providing a variance of opinion about falling and rising levels of achievement, who controls them and their implications for UK education in a competitive global market. Linked to the standards debate is the use of qualifications as performance indicators and the role of inspection processes in defining levels of performance: two often contentious areas of assessment practice. Finally, the use of assessment for *selection* purposes determines the manner in which society values achievement and raises questions about the criteria guiding such important decision-making processes.

The history of the major developments in assessment and qualification reform over the last 20 years is traced in Chapter 9 as an illustration of the key points underpinning current and future 14–19 and adult learning reforms. These reforms have the potential to create a standardized, unitized credit framework across the sector and this is reconsidered having been introduced in Chapter 1. Developments in electronic assessment are discussed as the area in which most future innovation in assessment is likely to occur.

## Conclusion

A series of core issues has emerged in the course of this book, which currently affect the assessment of FE students and will continue to do so. Perhaps the most important is that the way in which qualifications are structured and offered does not currently enable learners to follow clear progression paths, either vertically, from one level to another, or horizontally, across academic/vocational or career divisions. There has been no clear evidence that GCSE articulates with AS or A level and there was confusion around the level, status and relationship between AS and A level on the one hand and between this academic route and supposedly equivalent vocational GCSEs and vocational A levels in the Curriculum 2000 reforms. The introduction of the 14 specialized diploma lines does not promise to enhance such progression. There is no clear thinking by policy makers about how GCSE and A level will sit in or with the diplomas. And there is no certainty that a new Qualification and Credit Framework will offer a means by which such progression across the sector will be enabled.

There is continual public debate about the standards achieved by those taking GCSE and A level and a crisis of confidence on the part of both employers and higher education institutions in their efficacy in selecting students for employment or university. The irony is that A levels were never, any more than the School Certificate they replaced in 1951, intended to play this selective role and there is no convincing evidence that A level achievement is at all reliable as an indicator of effective study at degree level. There is some evidence that HEIs will move (as many already are and Oxbridge colleges always have) towards either their own assessment for selection or that a national scheme will emerge which separates the summative assessment of secondary level from assessment for selection for HE, as with the SATs or Scholastic Aptitude Tests in the United States. Equally ironic is that such a crisis in the public examinations system could come at a time of unprecedented credentialism, when the possession of qualifications is perceived as an important measure of ability, academic, vocational and professional.

The need for assessment *for* learning, as well as *of* learning, has been at the centre of major policy developments across education sectors, not just in FE. This follows the recognition that assessment has an important part to play in learning rather than a summative event separate from it. Recent developments in teacher education (the reform of initial teacher training, Centres for Excellence in Teacher Training and the Subject Learning Coaches Award) have all emphasized the importance of FE teachers' knowledge and understanding of pedagogy in their subject areas, including how assessment can enhance learning.

With over 3.5 million FE students, a steady increase from 2001–06, and 40 per cent of 16–18 year olds in FE as opposed to 30 per cent in maintained schools (www.dfes.gov.uk/trends), the FE population has never been a larger or more diverse body of students. Along with the necessity for teachers to differentiate according to learning needs is the equally important requirement that teachers offer students assessment opportunities that will best enable them to demonstrate their achievement. As suggested above, it is likely that developments in electronic assessment both by FE teachers, colleges, employers and awarding bodies will give students access to a wider range of strategies for doing so.

# Bibliography

Allen, K. (2007) 'It's arrived: feminisation of the net', *Guardian*, 23 August.

Andalo, D. (2007) 'Watchdog expresses concern over exam cheat', Guardian Unlimited, http://education.guardian.co.uk/schools/story/0,,2035046,00.html

Armitage, A., Byrant, R., Dunnill, R., Flanagan, K. and Hayes, D. (2007) *Teaching and Training in Post-Compulsory Education*. 3rd edn. Buckingham: Open University Press.

BBC News (2004) 'Student access benchmarks "flawed"', http://news.bbc.co.uk/1/hi/education/3746754.stm.

BBC News (2006) 'New students' skills "worsening"', http://news.bbc.co.uk/1/hi/education/4694714.stm.

BBC Radio 4 (2006) 'The good childhood enquiry'. Interview with Archbishop Rowan Williams broadcast 19 September.

Biggs, J. B. (1996) 'Enhancing teaching through constructive alignment', *Higher Education*, 32, 1–18.

Black, P. and Wiliam, D. (1998) *Inside the Black Box: Raising standards through classroom assessment*. London: School of Education, King's College.

Black, P., Harrison, C., Lee, C., Marshall, B. and Wiliam, D. (2003) *Assessment for Learning*. Maidenhead: Open University Press.

Bloom, B. S. (1956) *Taxonomy of Educational Objectives: Handbook 1/ Cognitive Domain*. London: Longman.

Butler, R. (1988) 'Enhancing and undermining intrinsic motivation: the effects of task-involving and ego-involving evaluation on interest and performance', *British Journal of Educational Psychology*, 58, 1–14.

Coffield, F., Hall, E., Moseley, D. and Ecclestone, K. (2004) *Learning Styles and Pedagogy in Post 16 Learning*. London: Learning and Skills Research Centre.

Dearing, R. (1996) *Review of Qualifications for 16-19 Year Olds*. Hayes: SCAA.

DfEE (2001) *Initial Assessment of Learning and Support Needs and Planning Learning to Meet Needs*. Sheffield: DfEE.

DfES (Department for Education and Skills) (2002) *14–19: Extending Opportunities, Raising Standards*. London: The Stationery Office.

DfES (2004a) *The Schwarz Review: fair admissions to higher education: the final review*, www.admissions-review.org.uk.

DfES (2004b) *14–19 Curriculum and Qualifications Reform* (Tomlinson Report). London: HMSO.

DfES (2005) *14–19 Education and Skills*. London: HMSO.

Ecclestone, K. (1996) *How to Assess the Vocational Curriculum*. London: Kogan.

Ecclestone, K. (2003) *Understanding Assessment and Qualifications in Post-Compulsory Education: principles, politics and practice*. Leicester: NIACE.

Edexcel (2003) 'Introduction to policy on electronic assessment', www.edexcel.org.uk/VirtualContent/59386/Policy_on_Electronic_Assessment.pdf

Follett, G. (2003) 'The place of assessment in quality enhancement in Scotland', *Exchange*, 4, Spring.

Foster, A. (2005) *Realising the Potential: A Review of the future role of further education colleges* (The Foster Report). London: DfES.

Gipps, C. V. (1994) *Beyond Testing: Towards a Theory of Educational Assessment*. London: The Falmer Press.

Guile, D. (2003) 'From "Credentialism" to the "Practice of learning": reconceptualising learning for the knowledge economy', *Policy Futures in Education*, 1, 1, 83–105.

Henry, J. (2006) 'A-level decline prompts switch to baccalaureate', *Telegraph*, 25 June, www.telegraph.co.uk/news/main.jhtml?xml=/news/2006/06/25/nedu25.xml.

Hodgson, A. and Spours, K. (2003) *Beyond A-levels: Curriculum 2000 and the Reform of 14-19 Qualifications*. London: RoutledgeFalmer.

Hodgson, A., Spours, K. and Wilson, P. (2006) *Tomlinson and the Framework for Achievement*. Leicester: NIACE.

Jones, C. (2005) *Vocational Learning Support Programme: 16–19 Assessment for Learning*. London: LSDA.

Klasen, N. and Clutterbuck, D. (2002) *Implementing Mentor Schemes*. Oxford: Butterworth Heinemann.

Lea, J., Armitage, A., Hayes, D., Lomas, L. and Markless, S. (2003) *Working in Post-Compulsory Education*. Milton Keynes: Open University Press.

Leitch Review of Skills (2006) *Prosperity for All in the Global Economy – World Class Skills* (Final Report). London: HM Treasury. www.dfes.gov.uk/skillsstrategy/uploads/documents/Leitch%20Review.pdf

Lightfoot, L. (2006a) 'Spoon-fed pupils can't cope at college', Tele-
graph.co.uk, 9 February, www.telegraph.co.uk/news/main.jhtm
l?xml=/news/2006/02/09/nedu09.xml.

Lightfoot, L. (2006b) 'State pupil numbers at university are going down',
Telegraph.co.uk, 21 August, www.telegraph.co.uk/news/main.jhtm
l?xml=/news/2006/07/20/nuni20.xml.

LLUK (2006) *New Overarching Professional Standards for Teachers, Tutors
and Trainers in the Lifelong Learning Sector*. London: LLUK.

LSC (Learning and Skills Council) (2007) 'Record success rates in further
education' April 17, www.lsc.gov.uk/news/latestnews/news-1704
2007.htm.

MacLeod, D. (2005) 'Let battle commence', Guardian Unlimited,
15 August, http://educationguardian.co.uk/alevels/story/0,,1549545,
00.html.

Martinez, P. and Munday, F. (1998) *9000 Voices: Student Persistence and
Drop-out in Further Education*. London: FEDA.

McAlpine, M. (2006) 'Using wikis to assess collaborative achievement',
www.futurelab.org.uk/resources/publications_reports_articles/web_
articles/Web_Article464

Nuffield Foundation (2006) 'The Nuffield 14-19 Review of learning',
www.nuffield14-19review.org.uk

Petty, G. (2004) *Teaching Today; a practical guide*. 3rd edn. Cheltenham:
Stanley Thornes.

QAA (Quality Assurance Agency for higher education) (2005) *Enhancing
Practice: Reflections on Assessment: Volume II*. QAA. www.enhancement
themes.ac.uk/documents/assessment/Reflections_on_Assessment_
Volume_2FINAL.pdf.

QCA (Qualifications and Curriculum Authority) (2002) *A summary of the
MORI/CDELL project in Spring 2002*. London: QCA. www.qca.org.
uk/qca_7673.aspx

Race, P. (2005) *Making Learning Happen: a guide for post-compulsory education*. London: Sage Publications.

Race, P., Brown, S. and Smith, B. (2005) *500 Tips on Assessment*. 2nd
edn. Abingdon: RoutledgeFalmer.

Robson, K. (2005) 'Assessment – The final frontier – Just how valid,
reliable and fair are assessments of disabled students?', *Enhancing
Practice: Reflections on Assessment: Volume II*. QAA, pp 84–90.
www.enhancementthemes.ac.uk/documents/assessment/
Reflections_on_Assessment_Volume_2FINAL.pdf.

Rogers, A. (1996) *Teaching Adults*. Buckingham: Open University Press.

Rowntree, D. (1987) *Assessing Students: How Shall We Know Them?*.
London: Kogan Page.

Scottish Qualifications Authority www.sqa.org.uk.files_ccc_CustConf 2007_SQAE_assessment.pdf

Tomlinson, S. (2001) *Education in a Post-welfare Society*. Buckingham: Open University Press.

Torrance, H. (2004) *Do Summative Assessment and Testing have a Positive or Negative Effect on Post-16 Learners' Motivation for Learning in the Learning and Skills Sector: a review of the research literature on assessment in the UK*. London: Learning and Skills Research Centre.

Torrance, H. (2005) *The Impact of Different Methods of Assessment on Achievement and Progress in the Learning and Skills Sector*. London: Learning and Skills Research Centre.

Tummons, J. (2005) *Assessing Learning in Further Education*. Exeter: Learning Matters Ltd.

Weyers, M. (2006) *Teaching the FE Curriculum* (The Essential FE Toolkit Series). London: Continuum.

Wolf, A. (2000) *Competence-based Assessment*. Buckingham: Open University Press.

Wolf, A. (2002) *Does Education Matter: myths about education and economic growth*. London: Penguin Business.

Working Group on 14-19 Reform (2004) *The Final Report on 14-19 Curriculum and Qualifications Reform* (The Tomlinson Report). London: Working Group on 14-19 Reform.

Wragg, T. (2005) 'Open up A-level debate', Guardian Unlimited, 18 August, http://education.guardian.co.uk/alevels/story/0,,1550943,00.html

## Websites

| | |
|---|---|
| http://arg.educ.cam.ac.uk | Assessment Reform Group |
| http://basic-skills.co.uk/ | The Basic Skills Agency is the national development organization for literacy and numeracy |
| www.aqa.org.uk | Assessment and Qualifications Alliance |
| www.dfes.gov.uk/14-19/ | DfES 14-19 |
| www.edexcel.org.uk | Edexcel Examining Board |
| www.ioea.org.uk | Institute of Educational Assessors |
| www.lifelonglearninguk.org | Lifelong Learning UK |
| www.lsda.org.uk/files/ pdf/2000015.PDF | A Learning and Skills Development Agency evaluation of initial assessment materials |
| www.ocr.org.uk | Oxford Cambridge and Royal Society of Arts Examining Board |
| www.psychtesting.org.uk | The British Psychological Society's Testing Centre |
| www.qca.org.uk | Qualifications and Curriculum Authority |
| www.sflqi.org.uk/index.htm | LSC's Skills for Life Quality Initiative |

# Index